Certified Internal Auditor Exam
Part 1

SECRETS

Study Guide
Your Key to Exam Success

CIA Test Review for the
Certified Internal Auditor Exam

Dear Future Exam Success Story:

First of all, **THANK YOU** for purchasing Mometrix study materials!

Second, congratulations! You are one of the few determined test-takers who are committed to doing whatever it takes to excel on your exam. **You have come to the right place.** We developed these study materials with one goal in mind: to deliver you the information you need in a format that's concise and easy to use.

In addition to optimizing your guide for the content of the test, we've outlined our recommended steps for breaking down the preparation process into small, attainable goals so you can make sure you stay on track.

We've also analyzed the entire test-taking process, identifying the most common pitfalls and showing how you can overcome them and be ready for any curveball the test throws you.

Standardized testing is one of the biggest obstacles on your road to success, which only increases the importance of doing well in the high-pressure, high-stakes environment of test day. Your results on this test could have a significant impact on your future, and this guide provides the information and practical advice to help you achieve your full potential on test day.

Your success is our success

We would love to hear from you! If you would like to share the story of your exam success or if you have any questions or comments in regard to our products, please contact us at **800-673-8175** or **support@mometrix.com**.

Thanks again for your business and we wish you continued success!

Sincerely,
The Mometrix Test Preparation Team

Need more help? Check out our flashcards at: http://MometrixFlashcards.com/CIA

Copyright © 2020 by Mometrix Media LLC. All rights reserved.
Written and edited by the Mometrix Exam Secrets Test Prep Team
Printed in the United States of America

TABLE OF CONTENTS

Introduction

Thank you for purchasing this resource! You have made the choice to prepare yourself for a test that could have a huge impact on your future, and this guide is designed to help you be fully ready for test day. Obviously, it's important to have a solid understanding of the test material, but you also need to be prepared for the unique environment and stressors of the test, so that you can perform to the best of your abilities.

For this purpose, the first section that appears in this guide is the **Secret Keys**. We've devoted countless hours to meticulously researching what works and what doesn't, and we've boiled down our findings to the five most impactful steps you can take to improve your performance on the test. We start at the beginning with study planning and move through the preparation process, all the way to the testing strategies that will help you get the most out of what you know when you're finally sitting in front of the test.

We recommend that you start preparing for your test as far in advance as possible. However, if you've bought this guide as a last-minute study resource and only have a few days before your test, we recommend that you skip over the first two Secret Keys since they address a long-term study plan.

If you struggle with **test anxiety**, we strongly encourage you to check out our recommendations for how you can overcome it. Test anxiety is a formidable foe, but it can be beaten, and we want to make sure you have the tools you need to defeat it.

Copyright © Mometrix Media. You have been licensed one copy of this document for personal use only. Any other reproduction or redistribution is strictly prohibited. All rights reserved.

Secret Key #1 – Plan Big, Study Small

There's a lot riding on your performance. If you want to ace this test, you're going to need to keep your skills sharp and the material fresh in your mind. You need a plan that lets you review everything you need to know while still fitting in your schedule. We'll break this strategy down into three categories.

Information Organization

Start with the information you already have: the official test outline. From this, you can make a complete list of all the concepts you need to cover before the test. Organize these concepts into groups that can be studied together, and create a list of any related vocabulary you need to learn so you can brush up on any difficult terms. You'll want to keep this vocabulary list handy once you actually start studying since you may need to add to it along the way.

Time Management

Once you have your set of study concepts, decide how to spread them out over the time you have left before the test. Break your study plan into small, clear goals so you have a manageable task for each day and know exactly what you're doing. Then just focus on one small step at a time. When you manage your time this way, you don't need to spend hours at a time studying. Studying a small block of content for a short period each day helps you retain information better and avoid stressing over how much you have left to do. You can relax knowing that you have a plan to cover everything in time. In order for this strategy to be effective though, you have to start studying early and stick to your schedule. Avoid the exhaustion and futility that comes from last-minute cramming!

Study Environment

The environment you study in has a big impact on your learning. Studying in a coffee shop, while probably more enjoyable, is not likely to be as fruitful as studying in a quiet room. It's important to keep distractions to a minimum. You're only planning to study for a short block of time, so make the most of it. Don't pause to check your phone or get up to find a snack. It's also important to **avoid multitasking**. Research has consistently shown that multitasking will make your studying dramatically less effective. Your study area should also be comfortable and well-lit so you don't have the distraction of straining your eyes or sitting on an uncomfortable chair.

The time of day you study is also important. You want to be rested and alert. Don't wait until just before bedtime. Study when you'll be most likely to comprehend and remember. Even better, if you know what time of day your test will be, set that time aside for study. That way your brain will be used to working on that subject at that specific time and you'll have a better chance of recalling information.

Finally, it can be helpful to team up with others who are studying for the same test. Your actual studying should be done in as isolated an environment as possible, but the work of organizing the information and setting up the study plan can be divided up. In between study sessions, you can discuss with your teammates the concepts that you're all studying and quiz each other on the details. Just be sure that your teammates are as serious about the test as you are. If you find that your study time is being replaced with social time, you might need to find a new team.

Copyright © Mometrix Media. You have been licensed one copy of this document for personal use only. Any other reproduction or redistribution is strictly prohibited. All rights reserved.

Secret Key #2 – Make Your Studying Count

You're devoting a lot of time and effort to preparing for this test, so you want to be absolutely certain it will pay off. This means doing more than just reading the content and hoping you can remember it on test day. It's important to make every minute of study count. There are two main areas you can focus on to make your studying count:

Retention

It doesn't matter how much time you study if you can't remember the material. You need to make sure you are retaining the concepts. To check your retention of the information you're learning, try recalling it at later times with minimal prompting. Try carrying around flashcards and glance at one or two from time to time or ask a friend who's also studying for the test to quiz you.

To enhance your retention, look for ways to put the information into practice so that you can apply it rather than simply recalling it. If you're using the information in practical ways, it will be much easier to remember. Similarly, it helps to solidify a concept in your mind if you're not only reading it to yourself but also explaining it to someone else. Ask a friend to let you teach them about a concept you're a little shaky on (or speak aloud to an imaginary audience if necessary). As you try to summarize, define, give examples, and answer your friend's questions, you'll understand the concepts better and they will stay with you longer. Finally, step back for a big picture view and ask yourself how each piece of information fits with the whole subject. When you link the different concepts together and see them working together as a whole, it's easier to remember the individual components.

Finally, practice showing your work on any multi-step problems, even if you're just studying. Writing out each step you take to solve a problem will help solidify the process in your mind, and you'll be more likely to remember it during the test.

Modality

Modality simply refers to the means or method by which you study. Choosing a study modality that fits your own individual learning style is crucial. No two people learn best in exactly the same way, so it's important to know your strengths and use them to your advantage.

For example, if you learn best by visualization, focus on visualizing a concept in your mind and draw an image or a diagram. Try color-coding your notes, illustrating them, or creating symbols that will trigger your mind to recall a learned concept. If you learn best by hearing or discussing information, find a study partner who learns the same way or read aloud to yourself. Think about how to put the information in your own words. Imagine that you are giving a lecture on the topic and record yourself so you can listen to it later.

For any learning style, flashcards can be helpful. Organize the information so you can take advantage of spare moments to review. Underline key words or phrases. Use different colors for different categories. Mnemonic devices (such as creating a short list in which every item starts with the same letter) can also help with retention. Find what works best for you and use it to store the information in your mind most effectively and easily.

Copyright © Mometrix Media. You have been licensed one copy of this document for personal use only. Any other reproduction or redistribution is strictly prohibited. All rights reserved.

Secret Key #3 – Practice the Right Way

Your success on test day depends not only on how many hours you put into preparing, but also on whether you prepared the right way. It's good to check along the way to see if your studying is paying off. One of the most effective ways to do this is by taking practice tests to evaluate your progress. Practice tests are useful because they show exactly where you need to improve. Every time you take a practice test, pay special attention to these three groups of questions:

- The questions you got wrong
- The questions you had to guess on, even if you guessed right
- The questions you found difficult or slow to work through

This will show you exactly what your weak areas are, and where you need to devote more study time. Ask yourself why each of these questions gave you trouble. Was it because you didn't understand the material? Was it because you didn't remember the vocabulary? Do you need more repetitions on this type of question to build speed and confidence? Dig into those questions and figure out how you can strengthen your weak areas as you go back to review the material.

Additionally, many practice tests have a section explaining the answer choices. It can be tempting to read the explanation and think that you now have a good understanding of the concept. However, an explanation likely only covers part of the question's broader context. Even if the explanation makes sense, **go back and investigate** every concept related to the question until you're positive you have a thorough understanding.

As you go along, keep in mind that the practice test is just that: practice. Memorizing these questions and answers will not be very helpful on the actual test because it is unlikely to have any of the same exact questions. If you only know the right answers to the sample questions, you won't be prepared for the real thing. **Study the concepts** until you understand them fully, and then you'll be able to answer any question that shows up on the test.

It's important to wait on the practice tests until you're ready. If you take a test on your first day of study, you may be overwhelmed by the amount of material covered and how much you need to learn. Work up to it gradually.

On test day, you'll need to be prepared for answering questions, managing your time, and using the test-taking strategies you've learned. It's a lot to balance, like a mental marathon that will have a big impact on your future. Like training for a marathon, you'll need to start slowly and work your way up. When test day arrives, you'll be ready.

Start with the strategies you've read in the first two Secret Keys—plan your course and study in the way that works best for you. If you have time, consider using multiple study resources to get different approaches to the same concepts. It can be helpful to see difficult concepts from more than one angle. Then find a good source for practice tests. Many times, the test website will suggest potential study resources or provide sample tests.

Copyright © Mometrix Media. You have been licensed one copy of this document for personal use only. Any other reproduction or redistribution is strictly prohibited. All rights reserved.

Practice Test Strategy

If you're able to find at least three practice tests, we recommend this strategy:

1. Take the first test with no time constraints and with your notes and study guide handy. Take your time and focus on applying the strategies you've learned.
2. Take the second practice test open-book as well, but set a timer and practice pacing yourself to finish in time.
3. Take any other practice tests as if it were test day. Set a timer and put away your study materials. Sit at a table or desk in a quiet room, imagine yourself at the testing center, and answer questions as quickly and accurately as possible.
4. Keep repeating step 3 on a regular basis until you run out of practice tests or it's time for the actual test. Your mind will be ready for the schedule and stress of test day, and you'll be able to focus on recalling the material you've learned.

Copyright © Mometrix Media. You have been licensed one copy of this document for personal use only. Any other reproduction or redistribution is strictly prohibited. All rights reserved.

Secret Key #4 – Pace Yourself

Once you're fully prepared for the material on the test, your biggest challenge on test day will be managing your time. Just knowing that the clock is ticking can make you panic even if you have plenty of time left. Work on pacing yourself so you can build confidence against the time constraints of the exam. Pacing is a difficult skill to master, especially in a high-pressure environment, so **practice is vital**.

Set time expectations for your pace based on how much time is available. For example, if a section has 60 questions and the time limit is 30 minutes, you know you have to average 30 seconds or less per question in order to answer them all. Although 30 seconds is the hard limit, set 25 seconds per question as your goal, so you reserve extra time to spend on harder questions. When you budget extra time for the harder questions, you no longer have any reason to stress when those questions take longer to answer.

Don't let this time expectation distract you from working through the test at a calm, steady pace, but keep it in mind so you don't spend too much time on any one question. Recognize that taking extra time on one question you don't understand may keep you from answering two that you do understand later in the test. If your time limit for a question is up and you're still not sure of the answer, mark it and move on, and come back to it later if the time and the test format allow. If the testing format doesn't allow you to return to earlier questions, just make an educated guess; then put it out of your mind and move on.

On the easier questions, be careful not to rush. It may seem wise to hurry through them so you have more time for the challenging ones, but it's not worth missing one if you know the concept and just didn't take the time to read the question fully. Work efficiently but make sure you understand the question and have looked at all of the answer choices, since more than one may seem right at first.

Even if you're paying attention to the time, you may find yourself a little behind at some point. You should speed up to get back on track, but do so wisely. Don't panic; just take a few seconds less on each question until you're caught up. Don't guess without thinking, but do look through the answer choices and eliminate any you know are wrong. If you can get down to two choices, it is often worthwhile to guess from those. Once you've chosen an answer, move on and don't dwell on any that you skipped or had to hurry through. If a question was taking too long, chances are it was one of the harder ones, so you weren't as likely to get it right anyway.

On the other hand, if you find yourself getting ahead of schedule, it may be beneficial to slow down a little. The more quickly you work, the more likely you are to make a careless mistake that will affect your score. You've budgeted time for each question, so don't be afraid to spend that time. Practice an efficient but careful pace to get the most out of the time you have.

Copyright © Mometrix Media. You have been licensed one copy of this document for personal use only. Any other reproduction or redistribution is strictly prohibited. All rights reserved.

Secret Key #5 – Have a Plan for Guessing

When you're taking the test, you may find yourself stuck on a question. Some of the answer choices seem better than others, but you don't see the one answer choice that is obviously correct. What do you do?

The scenario described above is very common, yet most test takers have not effectively prepared for it. Developing and practicing a plan for guessing may be one of the single most effective uses of your time as you get ready for the exam.

In developing your plan for guessing, there are three questions to address:

- When should you start the guessing process?
- How should you narrow down the choices?
- Which answer should you choose?

When to Start the Guessing Process

Unless your plan for guessing is to select C every time (which, despite its merits, is not what we recommend), you need to leave yourself enough time to apply your answer elimination strategies. Since you have a limited amount of time for each question, that means that if you're going to give yourself the best shot at guessing correctly, you have to decide quickly whether or not you will guess.

Of course, the best-case scenario is that you don't have to guess at all, so first, see if you can answer the question based on your knowledge of the subject and basic reasoning skills. Focus on the key words in the question and try to jog your memory of related topics. Give yourself a chance to bring the knowledge to mind, but once you realize that you don't have (or you can't access) the knowledge you need to answer the question, it's time to start the guessing process.

It's almost always better to start the guessing process too early than too late. It only takes a few seconds to remember something and answer the question from knowledge. Carefully eliminating wrong answer choices takes longer. Plus, going through the process of eliminating answer choices can actually help jog your memory.

Summary: Start the guessing process as soon as you decide that you can't answer the question based on your knowledge.

Copyright © Mometrix Media. You have been licensed one copy of this document for personal use only. Any other reproduction or redistribution is strictly prohibited. All rights reserved.

How to Narrow Down the Choices

The next chapter in this book (**Test-Taking Strategies**) includes a wide range of strategies for how to approach questions and how to look for answer choices to eliminate. You will definitely want to read those carefully, practice them, and figure out which ones work best for you. Here though, we're going to address a mindset rather than a particular strategy.

Your chances of guessing an answer correctly depend on how many options you are choosing from.

How many choices you have	How likely you are to guess correctly
5	20%
4	25%
3	33%
2	50%
1	100%

You can see from this chart just how valuable it is to be able to eliminate incorrect answers and make an educated guess, but there are two things that many test takers do that cause them to miss out on the benefits of guessing:

- Accidentally eliminating the correct answer
- Selecting an answer based on an impression

We'll look at the first one here, and the second one in the next section.

To avoid accidentally eliminating the correct answer, we recommend a thought exercise called **the $5 challenge**. In this challenge, you only eliminate an answer choice from contention if you are willing to bet $5 on it being wrong. Why $5? Five dollars is a small but not insignificant amount of money. It's an amount you could afford to lose but wouldn't want to throw away. And while losing $5 once might not hurt too much, doing it twenty times will set you back $100. In the same way, each small decision you make—eliminating a choice here, guessing on a question there—won't by itself impact your score very much, but when you put them all together, they can make a big difference. By holding each answer choice elimination decision to a higher standard, you can reduce the risk of accidentally eliminating the correct answer.

The $5 challenge can also be applied in a positive sense: If you are willing to bet $5 that an answer choice *is* correct, go ahead and mark it as correct.

Summary: Only eliminate an answer choice if you are willing to bet $5 that it is wrong.

Copyright © Mometrix Media. You have been licensed one copy of this document for personal use only. Any other reproduction or redistribution is strictly prohibited. All rights reserved.

Which Answer to Choose

You're taking the test. You've run into a hard question and decided you'll have to guess. You've eliminated all the answer choices you're willing to bet $5 on. Now you have to pick an answer. Why do we even need to talk about this? Why can't you just pick whichever one you feel like when the time comes?

The answer to these questions is that if you don't come into the test with a plan, you'll rely on your impression to select an answer choice, and if you do that, you risk falling into a trap. The test writers know that everyone who takes their test will be guessing on some of the questions, so they intentionally write wrong answer choices to seem plausible. You still have to pick an answer though, and if the wrong answer choices are designed to look right, how can you ever be sure that you're not falling for their trap? The best solution we've found to this dilemma is to take the decision out of your hands entirely. Here is the process we recommend:

Once you've eliminated any choices that you are confident (willing to bet $5) are wrong, select the first remaining choice as your answer.

Whether you choose to select the first remaining choice, the second, or the last, the important thing is that you use some preselected standard. Using this approach guarantees that you will not be enticed into selecting an answer choice that looks right, because you are not basing your decision on how the answer choices look.

This is not meant to make you question your knowledge. Instead, it is to help you recognize the difference between your knowledge and your impressions. There's a huge difference between thinking an answer is right because of what you know, and thinking an answer is right because it looks or sounds like it should be right.

Summary: To ensure that your selection is appropriately random, make a predetermined selection from among all answer choices you have not eliminated.

Copyright © Mometrix Media. You have been licensed one copy of this document for personal use only. Any other reproduction or redistribution is strictly prohibited. All rights reserved.

Test-Taking Strategies

This section contains a list of test-taking strategies that you may find helpful as you work through the test. By taking what you know and applying logical thought, you can maximize your chances of answering any question correctly!

It is very important to realize that every question is different and every person is different: no single strategy will work on every question, and no single strategy will work for every person. That's why we've included all of them here, so you can try them out and determine which ones work best for different types of questions and which ones work best for you.

Question Strategies

Read Carefully

Read the question and answer choices carefully. Don't miss the question because you misread the terms. You have plenty of time to read each question thoroughly and make sure you understand what is being asked. Yet a happy medium must be attained, so don't waste too much time. You must read carefully, but efficiently.

Contextual Clues

Look for contextual clues. If the question includes a word you are not familiar with, look at the immediate context for some indication of what the word might mean. Contextual clues can often give you all the information you need to decipher the meaning of an unfamiliar word. Even if you can't determine the meaning, you may be able to narrow down the possibilities enough to make a solid guess at the answer to the question.

Prefixes

If you're having trouble with a word in the question or answer choices, try dissecting it. Take advantage of every clue that the word might include. Prefixes and suffixes can be a huge help. Usually they allow you to determine a basic meaning. Pre- means before, post- means after, pro - is positive, de- is negative. From prefixes and suffixes, you can get an idea of the general meaning of the word and try to put it into context.

Hedge Words

Watch out for critical hedge words, such as *likely, may, can, sometimes, often, almost, mostly, usually, generally, rarely,* and *sometimes.* Question writers insert these hedge phrases to cover every possibility. Often an answer choice will be wrong simply because it leaves no room for exception. Be on guard for answer choices that have definitive words such as *exactly* and *always.*

Switchback Words

Stay alert for *switchbacks.* These are the words and phrases frequently used to alert you to shifts in thought. The most common switchback words are *but, although,* and *however.* Others include *nevertheless, on the other hand, even though, while, in spite of, despite, regardless of.* Switchback words are important to catch because they can change the direction of the question or an answer choice.

Copyright © Mometrix Media. You have been licensed one copy of this document for personal use only. Any other reproduction or redistribution is strictly prohibited. All rights reserved.

Face Value

When in doubt, use common sense. Accept the situation in the problem at face value. Don't read too much into it. These problems will not require you to make wild assumptions. If you have to go beyond creativity and warp time or space in order to have an answer choice fit the question, then you should move on and consider the other answer choices. These are normal problems rooted in reality. The applicable relationship or explanation may not be readily apparent, but it is there for you to figure out. Use your common sense to interpret anything that isn't clear.

Answer Choice Strategies

Answer Selection

The most thorough way to pick an answer choice is to identify and eliminate wrong answers until only one is left, then confirm it is the correct answer. Sometimes an answer choice may immediately seem right, but be careful. The test writers will usually put more than one reasonable answer choice on each question, so take a second to read all of them and make sure that the other choices are not equally obvious. As long as you have time left, it is better to read every answer choice than to pick the first one that looks right without checking the others.

Answer Choice Families

An answer choice family consists of two (in rare cases, three) answer choices that are very similar in construction and cannot all be true at the same time. If you see two answer choices that are direct opposites or parallels, one of them is usually the correct answer. For instance, if one answer choice says that quantity x increases and another either says that quantity x decreases (opposite) or says that quantity y increases (parallel), then those answer choices would fall into the same family. An answer choice that doesn't match the construction of the answer choice family is more likely to be incorrect. Most questions will not have answer choice families, but when they do appear, you should be prepared to recognize them.

Eliminate Answers

Eliminate answer choices as soon as you realize they are wrong, but make sure you consider all possibilities. If you are eliminating answer choices and realize that the last one you are left with is also wrong, don't panic. Start over and consider each choice again. There may be something you missed the first time that you will realize on the second pass.

Avoid Fact Traps

Don't be distracted by an answer choice that is factually true but doesn't answer the question. You are looking for the choice that answers the question. Stay focused on what the question is asking for so you don't accidentally pick an answer that is true but incorrect. Always go back to the question and make sure the answer choice you've selected actually answers the question and is not merely a true statement.

Extreme Statements

In general, you should avoid answers that put forth extreme actions as standard practice or proclaim controversial ideas as established fact. An answer choice that states the "process should be used in certain situations, if…" is much more likely to be correct than one that states the "process should be discontinued completely." The first is a calm rational statement and doesn't even make a

Copyright © Mometrix Media. You have been licensed one copy of this document for personal use only. Any other reproduction or redistribution is strictly prohibited. All rights reserved.

definitive, uncompromising stance, using a hedge word *if* to provide wiggle room, whereas the second choice is a radical idea and far more extreme.

Benchmark

As you read through the answer choices and you come across one that seems to answer the question well, mentally select that answer choice. This is not your final answer, but it's the one that will help you evaluate the other answer choices. The one that you selected is your benchmark or standard for judging each of the other answer choices. Every other answer choice must be compared to your benchmark. That choice is correct until proven otherwise by another answer choice beating it. If you find a better answer, then that one becomes your new benchmark. Once you've decided that no other choice answers the question as well as your benchmark, you have your final answer.

Predict the Answer

Before you even start looking at the answer choices, it is often best to try to predict the answer. When you come up with the answer on your own, it is easier to avoid distractions and traps because you will know exactly what to look for. The right answer choice is unlikely to be word-for-word what you came up with, but it should be a close match. Even if you are confident that you have the right answer, you should still take the time to read each option before moving on.

General Strategies

Tough Questions

If you are stumped on a problem or it appears too hard or too difficult, don't waste time. Move on! Remember though, if you can quickly check for obviously incorrect answer choices, your chances of guessing correctly are greatly improved. Before you completely give up, at least try to knock out a couple of possible answers. Eliminate what you can and then guess at the remaining answer choices before moving on.

Check Your Work

Since you will probably not know every term listed and the answer to every question, it is important that you get credit for the ones that you do know. Don't miss any questions through careless mistakes. If at all possible, try to take a second to look back over your answer selection and make sure you've selected the correct answer choice and haven't made a costly careless mistake (such as marking an answer choice that you didn't mean to mark). This quick double check should more than pay for itself in caught mistakes for the time it costs.

Pace Yourself

It's easy to be overwhelmed when you're looking at a page full of questions; your mind is confused and full of random thoughts, and the clock is ticking down faster than you would like. Calm down and maintain the pace that you have set for yourself. Especially as you get down to the last few minutes of the test, don't let the small numbers on the clock make you panic. As long as you are on track by monitoring your pace, you are guaranteed to have time for each question.

Copyright © Mometrix Media. You have been licensed one copy of this document for personal use only. Any other reproduction or redistribution is strictly prohibited. All rights reserved.

Don't Rush

It is very easy to make errors when you are in a hurry. Maintaining a fast pace in answering questions is pointless if it makes you miss questions that you would have gotten right otherwise. Test writers like to include distracting information and wrong answers that seem right. Taking a little extra time to avoid careless mistakes can make all the difference in your test score. Find a pace that allows you to be confident in the answers that you select.

Keep Moving

Panicking will not help you pass the test, so do your best to stay calm and keep moving. Taking deep breaths and going through the answer elimination steps you practiced can help to break through a stress barrier and keep your pace.

Final Notes

The combination of a solid foundation of content knowledge and the confidence that comes from practicing your plan for applying that knowledge is the key to maximizing your performance on test day. As your foundation of content knowledge is built up and strengthened, you'll find that the strategies included in this chapter become more and more effective in helping you quickly sift through the distractions and traps of the test to isolate the correct answer.

Now it's time to move on to the test content chapters of this book, but be sure to keep your goal in mind. As you read, think about how you will be able to apply this information on the test. If you've already seen sample questions for the test and you have an idea of the question format and style, try to come up with questions of your own that you can answer based on what you're reading. This will give you valuable practice applying your knowledge in the same ways you can expect to on test day.

Good luck and good studying!

Copyright © Mometrix Media. You have been licensed one copy of this document for personal use only. Any other reproduction or redistribution is strictly prohibited. All rights reserved.

Copyright © Mometrix Media. You have been licensed one copy of this document for personal use only. Any other reproduction or redistribution is strictly prohibited. All rights reserved.

Comply with the IIA's Attribute Standards

Audit Director Responsibilities

Guidance to Staff

A director should have a written manual of the department's policies and procedures accessible to auditing employees. It should cover expectations of progress reports, travel duties, auditing methods, and the means of reporting audit results to the appropriate people. Also, holding regular staff meetings allows opportunity for questions and problems to be discussed while monitoring the alignment of activities with planned goals. Finally, it is imperative that the director conveys the necessity for an internal auditor to report any bias or impartial judgment he may have working in a particular area, as it is essential for the department to maintain objectivity.

Human Resources

The audit director must create job descriptions for his department, determine a method for qualifying candidates, develop an employee evaluation system, and provide training and continuing education opportunities. Ideally, he should want an audit staff that has diversified knowledge and skill sets, so that together the staff is competent in performing internal audits throughout the vast areas within an organization. Therefore, when hiring a new employee, the director should try to fill any gaps within his staff's knowledge base. Also, a candidate should be familiar with auditing standards and have experience in practicing auditing procedures. Additionally, he should understand accounting methods and management styles. His college transcripts should be obtained, and his reference and job experience verified. Criteria for hiring an entry-level audit member should include having strong organizational and communication skills. Providing employees with feedback on their job performance allows the department to operate more efficiently and productively. New employees should be evaluated soon after their hire date to correct any inadequacies and enforce good practices. Thereafter, reviews should be conducted at least annually.

Quality Control

To assess the department's effectiveness, the director must implement a quality control program. This would incorporate a system of supervising all aspects of an audit, beginning with the justification for selecting a job. Are resources well-spent doing an audit here versus in another area of the organization? Reviewing the audit plans and methods to be performed, as well as the accuracy of the results reported, are also necessary.

Internal and external assessments also help determine the department's effectiveness. Internally, staff members may do peer reviews that will provide the director with feedback on strengths and weaknesses of his employees. For more objective employee assessments, external reviews may be acquired from areas the employees have audited. Additionally, surveys given to the customers may ask them to rate their satisfaction with the auditing report, the appropriateness of the recommendations given, and the overall benefits attained.

Assurance Services

The service of an internal auditor is to provide an objective evaluation along with suggestions for improvement to a particular operation within an organization. With assurance services, the parameters of the audit are fully determined by the internal auditor. Typically, three parties are involved in this arrangement: the internal auditor, the party directly involved with the operation, and the party who will use the assessment. Consulting services are provided at the request of a

Copyright © Mometrix Media. You have been licensed one copy of this document for personal use only. Any other reproduction or redistribution is strictly prohibited. All rights reserved.

client. The parameters of the audit are subject to client approval. And finally, there are only two parties involved: the internal auditor and the client.

Professional Care

An internal auditor should always conduct his work diligently and competently, using his audit skills, experience, and training to the best of his ability. When providing consulting services, he should meet with the client to understand their needs and ensure they understand the policies and procedures of the audit activities. It is important that they both agree on the method and timeliness of reporting results. All auditing activities should be performed according to the Standards and free from any bias. Any possible fraudulent activities must be reported with the recommendation for further investigation.

Independence and Objectivity

If an internal auditor was responsible for a specific operation within the previous year, he should not provide any assurance services to that area, as his judgment is likely to be tainted. Another auditor would be assigned to the area. It would be acceptable, however, for him to perform consulting services. If a Chief Audit Executive (CAE) has responsibility over a function which requires assurance services, an outside auditing organization must oversee the auditing activities. If consulting services have been conducted within the year prior to the necessity of assurance services, objectivity would be deemed impaired and this fact should be disclosed. To minimize biasness, different auditors and supervisors from the previous engagement should be assigned.

Long-Range Audit Plan

A long-range audit plan should coincide with the charter's objectives. More specifically, it should include an auditing schedule for the year that gives the beginning date for each area to be audited with an approximate ending date. Determining the order in which areas are to be audited must be prioritized based on the risk/benefit factors, previous audit results, and whether there have been major operating changes. The director's plan must consider staffing requirements and account for any necessary training or continuing education. Periodically, the director must report the department's status to management and the board. Progress may be shown with a comparative analysis of planned number and locations to be audited versus actual number and locations audited.

Audit Reports

The department manual should list, by job-title, the necessary attendees of the opening and closing audit conferences and detail the handling of both interim and final reports. Reports are allowed to express and auditor's opinion provided it is based on factual findings and is intended for improved results. The audit director, or someone he designated, is responsible for reading, approving, signing, and distributing all final audit reports. Also, it is his duty to revisit areas that have received their reports and to determine if recommendations are being followed and with what degree of success. If an audit uncovers illegal practices carried out by executive management, the report must be extended to the board of directors' audit committee.

International Standards for the Professional Practice of Internal Auditing

The purposes of the Standards are for recording the ideal procedures for internal auditing, establishing a guide for conducting internal auditing activities, providing a benchmark to assess internal auditing practices, and to encourage the improvements of organizational operations.

Copyright © Mometrix Media. You have been licensed one copy of this document for personal use only. Any other reproduction or redistribution is strictly prohibited. All rights reserved.

These Standards are subdivided as the Attribute Standards, Performance Standards, and Implementation Standards. The Attribute Standards cover the characteristics of internal auditing organizations. Performance Standards discuss the purpose of internal auditing procedures and provide a means for assessing their practices. The Implementation Standards address particular internal auditing activities, providing each major type of activity with its own set of Implementation Standards.

The Standards may be found in the Professional Practices Framework, along with the definition of Internal Auditing and a Code of Ethics. Practice Advisories for the Professional Issues Committee give advice of how to apply the Standards in practice.

Chief Audit Executive

According to the Standards, the Chief Audit Executive and the Chief Executive Officer should have a "functional" relationship and an "administrative" bond. The audit committee, which maybe a few members of the board or the entire board, has an overarching authority on the CAE. They have the final vote on the appointment and salary or dismissal of the CAE. After annual reviews of the CAE's effectiveness, the committee may allow or reject any suggested yearly increases. Also, the internal audit charter is subject to their review.

The CAE is expected to report to the audit committee with his yearly audit plan and any supporting documentation which the committee must review and approve prior to its implementation. Throughout the year, he should notify them of finalized auditing results and resolutions. To maintain objectivity, their meetings should be held without the presence of management.

Their communication covers everyday business activities, such as: discussing audit plans and activities, budgeting, and fulfilling human resource duties. Naturally, communications are extended to the management within the areas that are in the process of an audit.

While the CAE is obligated to share the auditing department's plans with the CEO, the CEO is prohibited from putting limitations on the scope of audits. Likewise, the CEO may not enforce budgets that are restrictive to auditors' abilities to properly conduct their work.

Auditor's Opinions

An auditor may express one of the following opinions in regard to a firm's financial statements:

- Unqualified Opinion – This favorable opinion is given when an auditor has been able to gather sufficient evidence, supporting the judgment that the financial statements are accurate, follow generally accepted accounting principles (GAAP), and therefore fairly represent the company's financial state.
- Qualified Opinion – This opinion is expressed when an auditor feels the financial statements are mostly accurate and fair with a small exception of little importance. It may be due to an audit scope limitation or something that does not comply with GAAP.
- Adverse Opinion – This type of opinion is stated when material information in the financial statements is grossly inaccurate or misleading thereby not in accordance with GAAP nor providing a fair financial representation.
- Disclaimer of Opinion – This only occurs when an auditor is unable to assess the fairness of a firm's financial statements. This may happen due to limitations put on the audit scope, disallowing the collection of sufficient evidence or when auditors are not independent enough from the firm to provide an unbiased opinion.
- Unqualified opinions are commonly issued whereas the other three are rarely expressed.

- 17 -

Copyright © Mometrix Media. You have been licensed one copy of this document for personal use only. Any other reproduction or redistribution is strictly prohibited. All rights reserved.

Outsourced Services

The need to hire an outside auditing organization or an experienced professional from a specific field may come if the internal department's staff is lacking knowledge in a particular area. For example, if the staff requires someone with expertise in law, they may hire an auditor with the appropriate knowledge from an outside organization or a lawyer, depending on their needs. Other situations requiring a hired specialist include uncommon occurrences, as with a merger or a fraud investigation. Also, assigning value to certain assets, such as property or fine art, may require an expert.

As always, the utmost objectivity of those performing auditing activities is necessary. Therefore, before obtaining outsourced services, the CAE must determine if there are any current or previous relationships, whether financial, working, or personal, between the outside party and the board or organizational members, particularly upper management. To verify competency, the CAE should view the outsourced candidate's educational background and previous work experience. Contacting references may be helpful. Also, any professional licensing, certification, or memberships should be considered. An outsourced service may be selected by the CAE, upper management, or the board. However, it is the CAE's job to assess whether the outsourced candidate is competent and will be objective. If the CAE feels the candidate is not appropriate, his assessment must be shared with the board and management.

Auditor's Responsibilities

To reduce expenses, management may try to stretch its resources by asking internal auditors to adopt responsibility over certain operations. This is obviously less than ideal and should be avoided, as it jeopardizes the internal audit department's independence and objectivity. However, if the situation arises, the charter should be scrutinized for any restrictions or limitations to such a request, which subsequently should be brought to management's attention. If management persists or the charter makes no reference to such a situation, the feasibility of the request should be assessed. The assessment must consider the exact responsibilities to be given, the time period of the assignment, and the potential biasness it may cause in future auditing activities. The assessment results need to be shared with the management and the audit committee. If the assignment is approved, disclosures of the assigned non-auditing responsibilities, the relationship of the auditors to the one performing non-audit duties, and the possible compromised objectivity must be reported to the audit committee during an audit.

Standards

In 2002, a new standard was issued, stating that internal audit departments are required to be internally assessed on an ongoing and periodic basis and externally assessed at least once every five years. An external assessment suffices the requirement for periodic assessments for that year. These requirements should be adopted and accounted for in the CAE's Quality Assurance and Improvement Program (QA&IP), which is a comprehensive overview of all the policies and procedures in accordance with the Standards and the internal auditing department's charter.

Environmental Audit Department

Research shows that auditors from the environmental audit department report to their managers, who report administratively to the managers of the area being audited. This administrative bond is a poor one since it allows operations managers the opportunity to influence the auditors and have them produce more favorable assessments to boost their image. Thus, it endangers the department's independence and objectivity. The independence may be regained by having the CAE

Copyright © Mometrix Media. You have been licensed one copy of this document for personal use only. Any other reproduction or redistribution is strictly prohibited. All rights reserved.

get more involved with the chief environmental officer. The CAE should propose looking over the environmental audit plan and periodically assessing their independence and objectivity, either by ensuring the EH&S audit department's policies and practices comply with environmental, health, and safety laws and regulations or evaluating management's methods for complying with such legislations. The CAE may also evaluate their adherence to Standards and code of ethics issued by the IIA and the Board of Environmental, Health, and Safety Auditor Certifications (BEAC). The CAE should advise the audit committee of any significant risk discovered.

Accessing Personal Information

Organizations are legally required to disclose the purpose for needing any personal information prior to or at the time of collecting it. To use or dispense the information in any other way than the stated purpose is illegal, unless the individual has given the organization prior consent to do so. An internal auditor must be aware that accessing, reviewing, and using personal information during certain audits may be inappropriate or even illegal. Therefore, it is always best to consult the legal department before performing audit activities that involve the use of personal information.

Audit Engagement Records

There are situations when a third party may request access to audit engagement records, such as during criminal and civil legal proceedings, tax audits, or governmental and regulatory reviews. In regard to criminal litigation, all company records must be made accessible with the exception of those held under the attorney-client privilege. When access to engagement papers is granted, only copies of the specific documents requested should be given. In court cases requiring original documents, copies should be retained. Each document should be marked "Confidential" and noted that further distribution is prohibited without prior permission.

The internal audit department may educate and continually remind the staff on the risks of unauthorized access to their records. They should have written policies addressing the contents of engagement records, retention periods, the handling of external requests, when an audit should become an investigation, and procedures for legal investigations. All such policies are subject to review by the audit committee. Additionally, the audit charter should provide guidelines as to who may have access to audit papers. Departmental policies should list which positions in the department are responsible for maintaining control over and safeguarding departmental records, as well as, those allowed to request access to engagement records and the procedure for doing so.

Differing Audit Opinions

Since the chief audit executive (CAE) is ultimately responsible for all internal audits, he must develop policies and procedures to ensure his audit staff does not make judgments contrary to his professional opinions, thus causing a negative impact on the results. For example, if conflicting opinions on significant auditing issues arise between the CAE and an auditor on his staff, established procedures may direct the following steps for finding a resolution: discuss views using supportive facts, research and obtain more facts, seek a third party expert opinion, and if no resolution can be agreed upon then record the opposing views in the working papers.

Attorney-Client Relationship

As internal auditors conduct their fieldwork, they document their findings as evidence. However, if they discover an illegal activity or government regulation violation, an auditor's documentation of it could be used as evidence against the organization in a courtroom. This would obviously hurt in-house counsel's legal defense. Therefore, policies should be established for the proper handling of

Copyright © Mometrix Media. You have been licensed one copy of this document for personal use only. Any other reproduction or redistribution is strictly prohibited. All rights reserved.

questionable discoveries regarding legal issues whereby the corporate council is notified prior to any record of its existence. If procedures are established and followed correctly, the auditor may protect his discovered knowledge through the attorney-client privilege. To establish that privilege the following elements must exist: (1) a confidential (2) communication must be made (3) between "privileged persons" (4) for the purposes of the client to obtain and the attorney to provide legal services. Any documents made prior to the attorney-client relationship are not protected from disclosure.

Work-Product Doctrine

Some courts have recognized the self-critical analysis privilege. This allows an organization's self-assessing documents, such as auditing papers, to be excluded from proceedings. The reasoning behind this doctrine is that organization's do self-evaluations for the purpose of making sure they are following the laws, which is in the public's best interest. If self-assessments are to be used in court, organizations may stop doing them. However, this privilege is more apt to be overlooked when a government agency is the plaintiff, as it is assumed, they have a greater interest in enforcing the law. The work-product doctrine protects the confidentiality of documents that are products of work, including paper memos and computer programs, created by an attorney in preparation for a legal case. However, if there is a substantial reason for needing the information, which is otherwise unattainable, the documents will not be protected.

Company Information

When an outside party requests information, the internal auditor should check the organization's policies and procedures, the audit department charter, and the audit committee charter for guidance on the types of information that are allowed to be reported outside the organization, which outside people are authorized for receiving information, how to obtain authorization for reporting it, and related legal and privacy issues. The outside request may require an audit to be conducted. If the request is for information or a report that has already been documented, the auditor should review the material to verify that it is permissible for outside parties to view and modify it if it is not. Sometimes creating a new report from previously done work will suffice. Prior to handing over the information, a written agreement between the provider and user should be prepared. It should include the identity of both parties, the sources of information, including those who conducted the research, its intended use, copyright restrictions, and limitations on the disbursement of information.

False Imprisonment

Prior to conducting investigative interviews, interviewers (auditors) must be aware of individuals' rights under common law and the possible allegations disgruntled employees can make. This knowledge will help ensure proper procedures are followed. Employers have the right to interview an employee on company grounds about breaches in corporate policies. However, if the interview is inappropriately conducted, an employee may accuse his employer of false imprisonment, provided he can prove:

1. he was arrested or physically held against his will,
2. without any legal justification,
3. under the company's direction, and
4. for a malice purpose.

Copyright © Mometrix Media. You have been licensed one copy of this document for personal use only. Any other reproduction or redistribution is strictly prohibited. All rights reserved.

Defamation of Character

During an investigation, an employer may communicate allegations. These communications are protected, privileged information. The privilege is revoked, however, if the agent is knowingly conveying false information for spiteful purposes to an excessive number of people; in which case, a suit may be brought against the agent for defamation of character. If the communications were oral, they would be known as slander. If they were written, they would be known as libel. To prove defamation of character, one must prove the following: the particular words communicated were false, they were communicated to third persons, and the time and place of communication can be established.

Malicious Prosecution

Should a company decide to prosecute an employee, the employee may claim malicious prosecution. For the claim to be valid, the following must be proved:

1. The employer initiated a legal action for malice purposes (reasons other than for bringing the employee to justice),
2. without probable cause, and
3. the proceedings were dismissed in the employee's favor.

An employer's malice may be established by proving a personal conflict exists between the accuser and the accused or by proving that the company is making untrue statements or is withholding pertinent information. If an interrogation got out of control and the interrogator used threatening words or gestures and seemed physically capable of causing harm, the employee could claim he was assaulted. If physical contact, either harmful or offensive, was made, then battery was committed.

Prevention of Criminal Activities

As of November 1991, new guidelines were established for the federal sentencing of organizations involved in white-collar crimes. Penalties may be as high as hundreds of millions of dollars. However, these penalties may be reduced in correlation to the amount of due diligence an organization can prove it demonstrated in attempts to prevent and detect criminal activity prior to the incident. Internal auditors should inform management of the federal sentencing guidelines and help create or improve programs to ensure the requirements of due diligence are met. To demonstrate due diligence, organizations should, at a minimum do the following:

- Standards and procedures in company policies and make sure all employees are aware of them by distributing publications or holding mandatory training programs.
- Delegate compliance-enforcing responsibilities to high-level employees.
- Maintain a separation of duties, reducing the opportunities for illegal activities.
- Take reasonable steps for encouraging compliance, as by incorporating monitoring controls, having audits, and establishing a system for employees to anonymously report violations.
- Discipline violators
- Take corrective actions to prevent repeat offenses

All evidence must be properly tagged. It should include the initials of the investigator seizing the item, the date, and the identity of the hardware and operating system which produced it, when applicable. Magnetic disk surfaces should not be written on. Diskettes should be only labeled with a felt-tip pen or an attached label. Reel-to-reel magnetic tapes should be marked on the dull side of the leader, which is the first 10-15 feet tape. It is important to transport magnetic media in climate-

Copyright © Mometrix Media. You have been licensed one copy of this document for personal use only. Any other reproduction or redistribution is strictly prohibited. All rights reserved.

controlled environments, as it is sensitive to dust, smoke, and extreme temperatures and humidity. Also, strong magnetic fields, as emitted from metal detectors and x-ray machines, should be avoided.

Total Quality Management

The following is an overview of the U.S. General Accounting Office's eight-step approach to Total Quality Management (TQM):

1. Conduct quality assessments by interviewing customers to provide a balanced evaluation of audit reports, in regard to their usefulness and timeliness; auditors' job performances; and opinions of the department.
2. Train the CAE to better understand the TQM philosophy.
3. Form a quality council consisting of audit managers, supervisors, and staff members, which report to the CAE. They must first learn the TQM philosophy and methods before coordinating training sessions for the rest of the department.
4. Encourage teamwork during audits.
5. The council should create prototypes, exemplifying how the implementation of TQM tools in the work process will bring success. This is to gain support in adopting the new TQM methods.
6. Advertise the prototype's success.
7. Implement TQM throughout all audit department units and recognize units with successful adoptions of TQM methods to motivate other units.
8. Administer yearly audit quality reviews to rate a unit's success in adopting quality-improving methods.

Code of Ethics

The International Standards for the Professional Practice of Internal Auditing defines ethics as follows:

Code of Ethics: The Code of Ethics of The Institute of Internal Auditors (IIA) are Principles relevant to the profession and practice of internal auditing, and Rules of Conduct that describe behavior expected of internal auditors. The Code of Ethics applies to both parties and entities that provide internal audit services. The purpose of the Code of Ethics is to promote an ethical culture in the global profession of internal auditing."

If an IIA member or IIA certified professional does not follow the Code of Ethics, the deviant behavior is evaluated and a disciplinary consequence is determined based on the Institute's Bylaws and Administrative Guidelines.

Location

A code of ethics, or code of conduct, refers to the proper and improper behaviors within the organization's environment. Typically, they are written into the corporate policies, internal auditing policies, or conflict-of-interest policies. While they are custom-tailored to specific company cultures, there are some commonly found policies. The three most common ones require compliance with laws and regulations, upholding the confidentiality of sensitive company information, and refraining from conflict-of-interests. Since conflict-of-interests frequently arise, many companies elaborate on this policy, prohibiting employees from accepting gifts or money, as well as, lending or borrowing funds from customers or vendors. Also, they may stipulate that employees may not hire family members as suppliers.

Copyright © Mometrix Media. You have been licensed one copy of this document for personal use only. Any other reproduction or redistribution is strictly prohibited. All rights reserved.

Codes are more effective when they mention disciplinary consequences for violators. Management must create a program for monitoring employees' compliance with the code of conduct, and the audit committee must review the program. And ultimately the legal department, internal audit activity, or ombudsman institutes the program.

New Employees

By drawing attention to the code of conduct, a new employee will sense the importance the company places on it and will take it more seriously than if it was just tossed in with a packet of new-hire papers. By gaining the employee's respect for the code of conduct, a greater likelihood exists that he will comply with it, and thus the ethical culture will be strengthened by one more member. Possible ways of drawing attention to the code of conduct include providing a training class that has management participation and discusses acceptable and unacceptable behaviors, sending it to the employee with a personal letter from the CEO, holding a workshop with role-playing scenarios, or supplying videotapes covering the topic with CEO or upper management appearances. By involving the CEO or high-level managers in the introduction to the code of conduct, a certain level of respect is enforced. Also, it shows that all levels throughout the organization must follow the code of conduct.

Rules of Conduct

The Rules of Conduct cover four main characteristics expected to be upheld in the internal auditing profession: integrity, objectivity, confidentiality, and competency. With regard to integrity, work in this profession requires someone who is trustworthy and honest, someone who is not tempted to partake in illegal or inappropriate activities. By objectivity, it is meant that a person understands the importance of remaining objective, free from prejudice, and so refrains from relationships, activities, and accepting gifts that may evoke biasness. The essence of confidentiality is that the professional keeps sensitive information quiet and does not use it for personal again. Finally, competency requires the person adhere to the Standards while providing services with properly matched qualifications. Also, he should continually seek self-improvement through experience and continuing education courses.

Copyright © Mometrix Media. You have been licensed one copy of this document for personal use only. Any other reproduction or redistribution is strictly prohibited. All rights reserved.

Establish a Risk-based Plan to Determine the Priorities of the Internal Audit Activity

Inherent Risk

Factors to be taken into account when assessing inherent risk include:

- Applicable Laws and Regulations - Once they have been identified, their understandability and reasonableness must be evaluated. Laws and regulations that are unclear or have unrealistic requirements have a greater probability of noncompliance. Also, the dates of when the laws and regulations were established or modified should be noted, as new or recently modified laws and regulations are at greater risk of noncompliance since employees may be unaware of them.
- High-Risk Indicators - Auditors should be watchful for indicators, or "red flags", alerting them to high-risk potentials of noncompliance when they are observing activities and interviewing employees.
- Management's Commitment - If management is stable, aware of potential problems, willing to share its philosophy on controlling noncompliance, open to trying new approaches, and quickly responds to problems, the auditor would assess the environment as having a low risk of noncompliance. This assessment may be done by reviewing management's response to previous audits and by interviewing the management team.

Auditors should be aware of these high-risk indicators of noncompliance:

- Activities controlled by one employee
- Vacations and promotions refused by employees
- Inadequate record-keeping
- Refusal to hand over records
- Complicated transactions
- Employee acts annoyed and gives poor explanations to reasonable questions
- A pattern of the same contractors bidding
- Important activities contracted to third parties without inspection of their internal controls
- Activities involving large amounts of liquid assets or assets of personal use

Sources of Information

As opposed to data that is raw numbers and facts, information is meaningful numbers and facts. To be useful, it must be available, timely, accurate, and relevant. Sources of information include primary and secondary, as well as, internal and external sources. Primary information is firsthand from a direct source, whereas secondary information comes secondhand. Internal sources reveal customer, sales, product, financial, and other company information. External sources are tapped for information about competitors, markets, and economic conditions. Using both external and internal sources leads to more informed decision-making which increases the likelihood of obtaining desired results.

Evaluating Data

An internal auditor has several factors to consider when determining the extent to which information should be reviewed and evaluated. The importance of the audit area's function with

- 24 -

Copyright © Mometrix Media. You have been licensed one copy of this document for personal use only. Any other reproduction or redistribution is strictly prohibited. All rights reserved.

regard to the entire organization is one such factor. An area with greater responsibilities would require more in-depth analysis. An area with high-risk or poor risk management would also warrant further testing. If data sources are hard to access or are unreliable, more intense examination would be required. Also, unavailable industry comparables would necessitate the need for further evaluations using other standards. If the analyses of data lead to unexpected or illogical results, management should be questioned, and further analysis must be performed until an explanation for such results is reached. Should the unexpected results still have no explanation after more in-depth investigation, there is an error present, a significant problem, or a fraudulent act has been committed. Unexplained findings should be reported to the appropriate management.

Audit Evidence

Transaction Entry and Transaction Authorization

As audit evidence changes form, auditors must find new methods for auditing them. The following are traditional types of audit evidence found in information systems and how they have changed:

Transaction entry - *Traditionally*: Employees enter a transaction into a processing system. A hard-copy of the input remains. *Computerized*: Computerized applications allow transactions to be triggered automatically and so no hard-copy of the input exists. For example, a company's bank account may be set for automatic withdrawal for making utility payments.

Transaction Authorization - *Traditionally*: Supervisors review transactions and indicate their approval for processing by signing or initialing the transaction. *Computerized*: Computer application systems may automatically approve transactions meeting a predetermined set of criteria, such as acceptance of a customer order using credit within a predetermined price range. Electronic data interchange (EDI) systems are able to pick-up and store dates, times, and authorization codes automatically. Electronic authorization that is not automatic may be entered as a password or authorization code.

Processing Methods

As audit evidence changes form, auditors must find new methods for auditing them. The following are traditional types of audit evidence found in information systems and how they have changed:

- Processing Methods and Documentation - Traditionally: Transaction processing is manually done by people and simplified to minimize errors. Processing large volumes of data is rarely done; as such a task is difficult, timely, and expensive. A hard-copy of steps to follow is accessible. Computerized: Computer application systems electronically process transactions and are capable of performing complex processes accurately and quickly. Large volumes of data may be stored in a database and quickly processed, sorted, and reported in various formats. A hard-copy of the processing steps does not exist, as it is coded within the computer programming.
- Processing Supervision - Traditionally: Supervisors oversee processing to ensure it is done correctly and completely. Computerized: Monitoring controls are embedded in the computer application system, ensuring proper processing.

Copyright © Mometrix Media. You have been licensed one copy of this document for personal use only. Any other reproduction or redistribution is strictly prohibited. All rights reserved.

Evidence

As audit evidence changes form, auditors must find new methods for auditing them. The following are traditional types of audit evidence found in information systems and how they have changed:

- Hard-copy outputs - Traditionally: Processing produces physical outputs, such as reports or checks. Computerized: Computerized applications alleviate the need for hard-copy outputs by digitally displaying data, such as full reports or exception reports on computer screens and being capable of electronic transfers, as with making electronic payments with the use of an electronic fund transfer system (EFTS), thus removing the need for printed checks.
- Procedural Manuals - Traditionally: Written procedures for processing a transaction on a computer system. Computerized: More sophisticated computer environments provide help-screens or online documentation of the procedures.

Document Movement and Storage

As audit evidence changes form, auditors must find new methods for auditing them. The following are traditional types of audit evidence found in information systems and how they have changed:

- Document Movement - Traditionally: People carry or mail documents. Computerized: Computerized application systems code, compress, and electronically transfer data through telecommunication lines. This may be done using an electronic data interchange (EDI) system, electronic fund transfer system (EFTS), or electronic mail.
- Document Storage - Traditionally: Hard-copy documents are stored in filing cabinets and may be physically retrieved. Computerized: Computer files are stored on CDs, tapes, cartridges, and hard-drives. They are accessible with the use of computer-based record retrieval programs.

Segregation of Duties

As audit evidence changes form, auditors must find new methods for auditing them. The following changes are found in the audit evidence, segregation of duties, within an IS audit: Traditionally: tasks are divided among employees. Computerized: Tasks are still divided among employees, but also processing steps are divided among computer programs. To exemplify the division of tasks, one employee may be responsible for entering transactions while a different employee has the authorization to make changes to the transaction. To exemplify a division of processing steps, one part of the transaction may be processed by computer program A while another part is processed by computer program B. For example, a purchase order for restocking inventory may require one program to track inventory levels, recognizing the reorder point while another program electronically sends a purchase order to the vendor.

Management Override

Management override refers to a manager using his authority to take actions contrary to the typical policies and procedures for corrupt purposes. Examples of this include purposely misrepresenting the company's financial position to secure a bank loan or falsely testifying to a lawyer about the company's compliance with state regulations. Other examples are for direct personal gains, such as falsifying employee expenses or purchase orders. Management intervention refers to a manager using his authority to take actions contrary to the typical policies and procedures for appropriate reasons. The need for management intervention occurs if there are unusual circumstances or atypical transactions that the control system would not handle correctly. These actions are usually documented or disclosed.

Copyright © Mometrix Media. You have been licensed one copy of this document for personal use only. Any other reproduction or redistribution is strictly prohibited. All rights reserved.

Financial Misstatements

There are three types of errors due to either intentional or accidental financial statement misstatements: known errors, likely errors, and possible errors. Known errors are ones that have been detected. Likely errors are forecasted based on the number of known errors in similar samplings. Possible errors are statistically determined using the combined number of known and likely errors. When "possible errors" exceed allowable materiality levels, the auditor may do more fieldwork to reduce the uncertainty of possible errors, or he must provide a negative opinion in the audit report.

The materiality of errors is different with each individual audit and its function, whether it is a financial audit, IT audit, operational audit, or compliance audit. The level of materiality to be used in an audit must be mutually understood by the auditor and auditee. This level may be quantified by using a percentage of a particular value, such as total revenues, total expenditures, total assets, retained earnings, or income. According to research, a useful determinant is to consider errors that would affect income by more than 10% to be material, and those that have a less than 5% effect on income to be immaterial.

While quantitative materiality may be determined during audit planning, qualitative materiality can only be decided during the audit. Qualitative materiality includes corruption, noncompliance with legalities, or incorrect classification of an account. These types of errors must take intensions, purposeful or accidental, into account.

Copyright © Mometrix Media. You have been licensed one copy of this document for personal use only. Any other reproduction or redistribution is strictly prohibited. All rights reserved.

Understand the Internal Audit Activity's Role in Organizational Governance

Internal Audit Department's Charter

The charter should include the department's purpose, authority, and responsibility for conducting auditing activities while being consistent with the Standards and having approval by the board. The charter should include the department's objectives which may include the following:

- Verifying that financial information was obtained correctly and reported accurately.
- Determining if controlling functions are done within management's specifications.
- Confirming the existence of assets and evaluating the methods used to protect them.
- Reporting the result of audits to appropriate management and giving recommendations for improvements, if necessary.
- Authority: In addition, the charter must state the parameters in which the department is allowed to fulfill its duties, thereby maintaining that the internal auditing department has the right to access, without limitation, all relevant files, records, and employees necessary to conduct an audit.
- Responsibility: Finally, the charter clarifies that the internal auditing department is only responsible for evaluating organizational activities; they may not assume control over them.
- To ensure audits are done using due care with properly educated and certified personnel whom maintain professionalism.

Assessments

Typically, ongoing assessments are embedded in the policies and everyday practices such as through supervision, required reporting, and customer comments or evaluations, whereas periodic assessments are less frequent and more formal. The IIA's Quality Assessment Manual is commonly used as a guide for periodic assessments. They may be completed by internal audit staff members, an audit professional located elsewhere in the organization, or some combination thereof. They may use various methods (i.e., interviews, comparative analysis, surveys, testing) for the purpose of assessing the internal auditing activity's compliance with the Standards, the charter, and the IIA's Code of Ethics. Additionally, they are assessing whether the internal audit department is doing their work efficiently and providing effective results, thus adding value to the firm. Those conducting the assessments should have continuous communication with the CAE throughout the process and report final results to him.

External Assessments

External assessments should be done by an individual or organization that is independent, void of any interests or relationships associated with the hiring firm and its members, and professionally competent. More specifically, an external assessor should hold certification in the auditing field and have a minimum of 3 years of managerial experience in internal auditing. Additional qualifications for the assessment team leader include: passing the IIA's quality assessment training course, having prior experience as a member of an external assessment team, and previous employment as a CAE. When choosing an external assessor, the CAE must include upper management and the board, as their approval is required.

Copyright © Mometrix Media. You have been licensed one copy of this document for personal use only. Any other reproduction or redistribution is strictly prohibited. All rights reserved.

Purpose and Reporting

An external assessment evaluates a broad spectrum of internal auditing activity for the purpose of determining whether it is in compliance with the Standards, Code of Ethics, and the internal audit department's charter. The assessor should discuss findings with the CAE throughout the process.

The final assessment should contain the assessor's opinion with regard to the department's compliance with the Standards. Also, an evaluation of the department's efficiency and effectiveness along with any recommendations for improvement would be incorporated into the final assessment. The party who initially authorized the external assessment, usually the CAE, would receive the finalized report. The CAE should address, in writing, any strong suggestions or comments made. He is expected to formally communicate the results with upper management and the board.

Independent Validation

The IIA has made an allowance for small internal auditing departments to do a self-assessment with independent validation in lieu of the required external assessment. This self-assessment concentrates mainly on evaluating the internal audit activity's compliance with the Standards. The CAE heads an assessment team using the IIA Quality Assessment Manual to guide them throughout the process. After the self-assessment is documented with a preliminary report, resembling an external assessment, an external assessor must be brought in to test the validity of the self-assessment. He must be an independent, competent professional possessing the same qualifications as a team leader of an external assessment team. The external assessor finalizes the self-assessing report by adding his findings to support his professional opinion with regard to the internal audit department's compliance with the Standards. If necessary, recommendations are given. The external assessor and the self-assessment team sign the report which the CAE presents to upper management and the board.

Governance Process

Organizations have certain responsibilities to their employees, consumers, investors, and to society, in general. These responsibilities include abiding laws and regulations, adopting socially and ethically accepted business practices, reporting fully and honestly, and adding overall value. An organization's governance process is the established policies and procedures designed to meet those responsibilities. The process is directed by the board of directors, or equivalent governing body, and executive management. However, since the responsibilities are mostly ethical obligations, the success of the governing process hinges in the organization's ethical climate. Thus, the need exists for organizations to encourage ethical values.

Ethical Culture

Organizations try to foster a certain level of ethical consciousness. The internal audit department should periodically evaluate the ethical climate and the effectiveness of the firm's methods for achieving it. The auditor's opinions may be formed from determining if the written code of conduct is adequately and clearly conveying ethical and behavioral expectations; noting the frequency of which leaders are expressing the company's message and exemplifying the desired attitude; familiarizing themselves with company programs aimed at increasing or reminding employees of ethical expectations; reviewing surveys of ethics taken by the organization's personnel, suppliers, and clients; determining if the procedures for reporting possible violations are simplistic and confidential; and observing how investigations of alleged violations are conducted. Internal auditors may support the firm's ethical culture as an ethics advocate by serving on the internal

- 29 -

Copyright © Mometrix Media. You have been licensed one copy of this document for personal use only. Any other reproduction or redistribution is strictly prohibited. All rights reserved.

ethics council or becoming a chief ethics officer to counsel executive management on ethical decision-making.

Compliance Testing

While planning an audit, auditors must learn which laws and regulations apply to the function being audited. This information may be obtained from attorneys and relevant documentation. Next, the vulnerability of those laws and regulations falling prey to violation or abuse must be assessed. This vulnerability assessment takes two factors into account. First the inherent risk, or probability of an illegal act or abuse occurring, should be calculated. Then the likelihood of internal controls preventing or detecting the noncompliance or abuse should be factored in. As an equation, it appears as:

$$\text{VULNERABILITY} = \text{INHERENT RISK} \times \text{STRENGTH OF INTERNAL CONTROLS}$$

Therefore, an activity with an inherently high risk of noncompliance may not necessarily be assessed as highly vulnerable if strong internal controls exist. Areas that do have high vulnerability will require more in-depth compliance testing; the higher the vulnerability, the more extensive the testing.

Compliance Audits

Since government organizations are established under law and generally have more legal requirements and regulations to follow than organizations in the private sector, typically more compliance audits take place in the public sector. While assessing internal controls for a compliance audit, it is important for the auditor to be aware of the possible limitations that may hinder the control system's effectiveness. For example, costs may keep a control from being implemented if they exceed the potential benefits. Other limitations include employee collusion to circumvent controls, management's ability to override controls, and human error in following procedures due to misunderstanding them or being distracted or overtired.

Hazardous Waste Management Program

The procedures for auditing a hazardous waste management program include:

- Ensuring the program requires the following actions before the organization takes possession of real estate: acquiring information about all previous owners and how they used the property, and inspecting the real estate to verify it is contaminant-free.
- Understanding which products or by-products are hazardous.
- Researching methods to minimize the production of hazardous wastes.
- Confirming compliance with all government policies and standards regarding: clean air, clean water, and acceptable procedures for hauling and disposing hazardous wastes.
- Making sure the program requires someone to monitor current regulations and environmental standards so policies and procedures may be updated to meet any new requirements.
- Determining if insurance is adequate and reasonably priced.

Safety Program

While auditing an organization's human resource policies, auditors should assess the firm's safety program to ensure it complies with job safety standards created and enforced by the Occupational Safety and Health Administration (OSHA), a federal government agency. Their laws require

- 30 -

Copyright © Mometrix Media. You have been licensed one copy of this document for personal use only. Any other reproduction or redistribution is strictly prohibited. All rights reserved.

businesses with direct or indirect involvement in commerce to be responsible for: knowing the safety standards, maintaining a healthy and safe work environment, and educating employees on safety practices.

Successful safety programs require: management's commitment to the program, employee participation, and proper accident investigations. Since employers may be held legally liable for not enforcing safety rules, it is important to make managers/supervisors accountable for safety in their area by including it as a criterion on their job performance evaluations. Some firms also have a safety manager to analyze job safety, establish written safety procedures, train employees, and investigate accidents. Investigations are for discovering accident causes. Based on the results, future accidents may be eliminated by changing job procedures, adding safety precautions, or improving training techniques. They may also detect fraudulent worker's compensation claims.

Disaster Recovery Plans

A business continuity plan is designed to orchestrate the necessary steps to quickly resume business after a disaster. Internal auditors may assist in formulating these plans by helping identify, assess, and prioritize the risks associated with a disaster. Since internal auditors have a comprehensive understanding of the various components in the organization and how they interrelate during business operations, they are able to evaluate the plan's design, methodology for risk management and control processes, and overall thoroughness. Once the business continuity plans are established, internal auditors should periodically audit them to make sure they are updated, reflecting any major changes, particularly in key employees, business operations, or software. Any revisions to the plan must be communicated to the appropriate people. If a disaster occurs, the internal audit department may support recovery efforts. They should evaluate the adequacy of the recovery process and effectiveness of the controls and provide recommendations where improvements are needed. Knowledge gained from a disaster experience should go towards revisions in the business continuity plan.

Electronic Commerce

Electronic commerce, or e-commerce, refers to the transacting of business over the Internet. Since this is a rapidly evolving environment, the IIA Research Foundation has put out a publication, Systems Assurance and Control (SAC), to help internal auditors identify and assess risks associated with e-commerce. Examples of e-commerce related risks that internal auditors must assess include: government regulations, the security and dependability of the hardware and software, the accuracy of the transactions, the likelihood and opportunities for fraud, accidental or intentional data corruption, and possible business interruptions.

ABC Inventory Method

The ABC inventory method categorizes inventory items as A-class, B-class, or C-class items. A-class items have a high turnover rate and should be inspected monthly; whereas B-class items do not move as quickly and may be checked quarterly; and C-class items are the least-demanded, slowest moving items, requiring an annual count. This method helps maintain appropriate inventory levels for different items having varying levels of demand.

Copyright © Mometrix Media. You have been licensed one copy of this document for personal use only. Any other reproduction or redistribution is strictly prohibited. All rights reserved.

Inventory Turnover Rate refers to how much inventory is sold in a year. It is calculated by dividing the cost of goods sold by the year's average inventory. The year's average inventory is calculated by adding together the beginning and ending inventories and dividing by two.

$$\text{Inventory Turnover Rate} = \text{COGS/Average inventory}$$

$$\text{Average Inventory} = (\text{Beginning Inventory} + \text{Ending Inventory}) / 2$$

Order Point Technique

Order Point (OP) Technique is a system by which inventory items are ordered from a supplier when the inventory in stock falls to a predetermined order point. The reorder point is usually figured by determining the lead time demand, which is the quantity of products demanded during the time it takes to replenish the product stock and adding a desired amount of safety stock. As an equation, it appears as:

$$\text{Reorder Point} = \text{Lead time demand} + \text{safety stock}$$

Economic Order Quantity

Economic Order Quantity (EOQ) refers to the most economic quantity to order, taking into account the inverse relationship of ordering costs and storing costs. Ordering costs are the costs of order placement, delivery, and unloading; and storing costs are the costs associated with holding the inventory. If more items are ordered less frequently, ordering costs will decrease but storing costs will increase. If less items are ordered more frequently, storing costs will decrease but ordering costs will increase. Therefore, the EOQ is the amount that provides an optimal balance of these two types of costs.

Inventory Planning Techniques

Definitions are as follows:

- *Exponential smoothing*: a forecasting technique which allows recent observations to have a stronger impact on the forecast than older observations. This is accomplished by assigning weighted factors to each observation. The older the observation, the exponentially smaller weighted value it receives.
- *Materials Requirements Planning (MRP)*: uses a computer system, which monitors the inventory levels of all the raw materials used in the manufacturing of a finished product, to develop and maintain plans for purchasing and manufacturing production materials.
- *Regenerative MRP*: a system whereby materials used by the day's end are totaled and entered into a regenerative computer system which recalculates the entire projected materials needed for future production.
- *Net Change:* a computer program which updates only the areas that have quantitative or timing changes and their resulting effects.

Copyright © Mometrix Media. You have been licensed one copy of this document for personal use only. Any other reproduction or redistribution is strictly prohibited. All rights reserved.

Cost Accounting

The following defines different types of variances:

- Price variance is the difference between actual and standard price-per-unit, times the actual quantity sold.
- Efficiency variance is the difference between the actual and standard allowable inputs used, times the standard price per input.
- Production volume variance is the difference between expected and actual number of products produced, times the budgeted overhead rate per product unit.
- Lot size variance is the difference between actual and standard units in a lot size, times the standard unit setup cost.
- Scrap variance is the difference between the actual and allowable weight of scrap material, times the standard scrap price.
- Standard revision variance is the difference between old and new standards.

Financial Audits

The purpose of a financial audit is to express a professional opinion as to whether a firm's financial statements are accurate; conform with generally accepted accounting principles (GAAP); and fairly represent the firm's financial position.

The scope of the audit is primarily centered on accounting data, such as provided by the balance sheet, which reports the company's status at the close of the accounting period, and by the income statement, which shows earned income during the period.

Financial audits are performed by independent auditors from outside the firm. However, their work and the work of internal auditors may be mutually shared in the assessment of internal controls for compliance with company policies and procedures and overall adequacy.

Full Disclosure

Public corporations are required to fully disclose pertinent information that may influence investors' decisions on a regular basis. During a corporate takeover, the company must publicly disclose the offer made and all relevant facts in a timely manner to allow shareholders the opportunity to make informed decisions. Directors and employees are not allowed to personally gain from the use of company information that has not been disclosed to the public. That is considered insider trading. Other cases of insider trading have occurred from companies selectively disclosing inside information to security professionals and large investors. The Security Exchange Commission (SEC) put a stop to this with Regulation FD (fair disclosure) requiring any important information that is disclosed to investment professionals or shareholders be made public in fairness to small investors.

Sarbanes-Oxley Act

The Sarbanes-Oxley Act was created in response to corporate scandals that involved negligent acts by upper management and their accounting firms. Also, the statute of limitations on fraud has been increased to two years after the date of discovery and five years after the date of occurrence.

The Public Company Accounting Oversight Board, formed under the Act, consists of five members who collectively create standards for auditors of publicly–owned corporations. Their right to enforce those standards include: inspections of public accounting firms' auditing activities with

Copyright © Mometrix Media. You have been licensed one copy of this document for personal use only. Any other reproduction or redistribution is strictly prohibited. All rights reserved.

public corporations, as well as, determining the disciplinary and corrective actions for violators of board policies, auditing and accounting standards, and securities laws. They may impose financial penalties of $100,000 for individuals and $15 million for corporations.

To allow for opportunities of earlier detection of auditing and accounting problems or misdoings, the audit committee is expected to establish a system of receiving, investigating, and resolving employee complaints of such. The system must allow for employees to convey their complaints anonymously or confidentially.

To assign accountability for the quarterly financial statements, the Act mandates that the CEO and CFO must both certify to the statements' accurateness, to the existence of internal controls, and to disclosing any internal control issues to external auditors and the audit committee.

The Act also requires annual reports to have a statement explaining that the maintenance of acceptable internal controls and financial reporting procedures is management's responsibility. An assessment of the internal controls and report procedures along with an external auditor's confirmation of the assessment must also be included in the annual report. It further mandates a publicly-held company must allow public access to its code of ethics either through its annual report, its company website, or by request.

Due Diligence Audits

Due diligence audits are to ensure compliance with laws and regulations, and to assess risks and exposures during business acquisitions, mergers, and consolidations. These audits require teamwork among internal auditors, lawyers, engineers, information technology (IT) analysts, and any other required experts. There are three main phases in a due diligence audit. First, information must be collected through documents, records, and interviews. Next, analysis and statistical review of the information is completed. And finally, a written report is created with an accompanying summary. Oral reporting may occur throughout the process for auditors to obtain clarity on certain issues.

Operational Audits

Operational audits must review several areas to be comprehensive. Therefore, to manage the audit efficiently and effectively, related activities are grouped into the following divisions: revenue, expense, financing and investing, and financial reporting. Manufacturing firms have the additional division of production. Within each division are departments, each with its own set of preventive and detective controls, as well as, risks that the auditors must address in their objectives.

However, some controls and objectives apply to the entire operation. An example of such controls includes directive controls, such as organizational policies and procedures, job descriptions, and the organization's structuring. Objectives that deal with transactions, ensuring they are accurate and authorized, as well as, properly recorded, posted, reconciled, and reported, also apply across the operation.

Operating Divisions

Activities taking place in the revenue division of operations include receiving and processing customer orders, shipping, billing, extending credit, inventory updating, and recording transactions appropriately.

Copyright © Mometrix Media. You have been licensed one copy of this document for personal use only. Any other reproduction or redistribution is strictly prohibited. All rights reserved.

Activities of the expense division include vendor selection, paying vendors, issuing purchase orders, receiving and storing purchased goods, hiring employees, authorizing employee compensation, tracking employee hours and maintaining a payroll system.

The production division has these activities that should be included in an audit: tracking and protecting inventories of raw materials, works-in-progress, and finished goods; filling production orders; shipping finished goods; recording production transactions; maintaining equipment; and inspecting quality of work.

The financing and investing division handles these activities: issuing and repurchasing stock, paying dividends, issuing bonds, paying interest, paying principal at maturity, investing in securities, filing tax forms, creating and protecting transaction records.

The financial reporting division prepares financial statements which must abide with generally accepted accounting principles (GAAP).

Reviewing Accounting Estimates

There are various instances when an estimate is required in accounting, such as determining: uncollectible accounts receivable, obsolete inventory, and allowances for losses, to name a few. Since a subjective element plays a role in determining an accounting estimate, it is important for auditors to inquire about management's methods for deriving at their estimates and then to assess the reasonableness of the estimates. During such a review, auditors should approach the task with a professional skepticism, meaning they should not approach the review assuming management is completely honest nor purposefully dishonest.

Auditing a Contract

Contract audits should begin early in the process before a contract is signed. Internal auditors may assess cost estimates, determine risks associated with the contractual terms, and ensure effective cost and progress controls are in place, such as by making provisions in the contract for progress and billing reviews.

Fixed Price Contract – This contract agrees to complete a particular job for a set price. Risks: The promised quantity and/or quality of materials are not received. Additional charges are billed for excess labor or materials.

Cost-plus-fee Contract – In this agreement, a contractor is reimbursed for the costs of completing a project and receives an additional fee. The additional fee may be a percentage of total costs incurred, or more preferably, a fixed fee. Risks: Inefficient work practices result in excessive labor, materials, and overhead expenses.

Unit-price Contracts – In this arrangement an agreed upon price-per-unit of work is paid. Risks: Units completed may be incorrectly reported. The contractor may try to sneak in unauthorized price adjustments.

Quality Audits

Knowing that quality provides a competitive edge which may bring increased sales, revenues, and profits, successful companies keep close tabs on the quality of their products/services. Management relies on the audit and quality departments for assurance that resources are being used efficiently and effectively. Therefore, it is important to have quality audits of the

Copyright © Mometrix Media. You have been licensed one copy of this document for personal use only. Any other reproduction or redistribution is strictly prohibited. All rights reserved.

product/service quality department and internal audit department. The scope of a product/service quality department's audit should cover quality policies and procedures, quality management and control tools, quality standards, quality legalities, six-sigma metrics, and determining the costs of quality. Auditing this area requires a good understanding of how the various tools for quality management and control are used and applied, how six-sigma metrics are implemented, how quality costs are calculated, and how service quality characteristics are measured. Quality audits of the internal audit department are accomplished through the implementation of a total quality management (TQM) approach.

Evaluating Internal Controls

When evaluating internal controls, the auditor must first identify the policies and procedures management has established to ensure compliance with laws and regulations. Their effectiveness depends on the control environment. The control environment refers to the general attitude towards management and respect for the controls. Contributing factors that set this tone include: the organization's structure, as well as, management's philosophy and methods of supervising, delegating, and implementing corrective actions. Gathering information to form an opinion of the control environment may come from interviewing employees and management, as well as, from observations.

To determine if the internal controls are effective, the auditor should test a small sample of transactions to evaluate whether the laws, regulations, and internal controls were followed as the transactions had been processed. The results should be documented, and the probability of internal controls not being able to prevent or detect noncompliance should be determined. Further testing may be done in areas of weak controls so auditors may provide better suggestions.

Consolidated Omnibus Budget Reconciliation Act

The Consolidated Omnibus Budget Reconciliation Act (COBRA) of 1986 applies to organizations of twenty or more employees. According to this act, employers must offer continued group health insurance coverage for a specified time period to employees and their dependents under the following circumstances: employee termination, layoff, death, or a dependent turns an age that is no longer eligible for dependency status. Once the continuation period expires, the employee may convert his group coverage to an individual policy, which will have a higher premium. Auditors must ensure the organization complies with the requirements of notifying qualified individuals of COBRA and offering them continued group health insurance coverage for the specified time period.

I-9 Employment Eligibility

Auditors must make sure their organization complies with the Immigration Reform and Control Act of 1986 by having employees complete the I-9 Employment Verification form to verify they are U.S. citizens or aliens with authorization to work in America. If an alien cannot show evidence of having authorization to find American employment, an employer may withdraw its employment offer. Required Postings - Auditors must ensure that the required postings of federal and state labor laws are displayed in the workplace. These laws address the following employee rights: equal employment opportunities, minimum and overtime wages, family leave, medical leave, job safety, and health protection. Other required postings include notice of federally financed construction and federal government contracts.

Copyright © Mometrix Media. You have been licensed one copy of this document for personal use only. Any other reproduction or redistribution is strictly prohibited. All rights reserved.

Exit Interviews

Exit interviews take place when an employee is departing from the firm. A human resource representative meets with the employee to obtain company property that has been in the employee's possession and to explain benefits he is entitled to, such as COBRA, severance pay, and pension/retirement funds. More importantly, though, the representative interviews the employee to understand the reasons for his decision. This helps human resources control high employee turnover by identifying possible problems that may be fixed to prevent other employees from leaving. Such problems may include unacceptable working conditions, issues with other employees or management, or insufficient compensation. Auditors should ensure exit interviews are taking place, ideally with someone independent from the situation, and also that follow-up actions are based on the interviewees' input.

Other Policies

Telephone Usage - With regard to the use of company telephones, auditors should determine whether proper phone etiquette is being used and assess the effectiveness of controls preventing abuse of the phone line, such as the making of unauthorized long-distance and/or personal calls.

Smoking Policy - Auditors must ensure the company's smoking policy complies with city ordinances and OSHA regulations, which prohibit smoking near flammable items or substances in the workplace. He must also determine whether employees are respecting the policy by verifying smokers only smoke in the designated areas or not at all if the policy bans smoking. To help maintain compliance where it is banned, employees may be encouraged to attend a company-sponsored smoking clinic.

The U.S. Constitution prohibits government infringement upon individual rights, which means employees of the public sector are protected from unreasonable drug searches and drug tests by privacy rights. These rights do not apply within the private sector unless privacy provisions have been extended to that sector by a state constitution. Auditors should verify their firm's drug testing program complies with privacy rights and is effective.

Common drug-testing programs include one or more of the following:

- New-hire testing – A job offer may be contingent on passing a drug test.
- Reasonable Cause testing – Occupations involving the safety of others, such as passenger transportation drivers and nuclear power plant workers, are required to take drug tests.
- Random testing – Occasional, surprise testing is done to ensure employees are always drug-free. It catches drug users that have found methods for passing scheduled testings.
- Universal testing – A scheduled or unscheduled drug testing of all employees.

Inappropriate or excessive use of alcoholic beverages or drugs, including over-the-counter, prescription, or illegal drugs, constitutes substance abuse. Since increased absenteeism, errors, poor work attitude and productivity, and on-the-job accidents are common results of substance abuse, it is imperative to have a substance abuse policy. Auditors should ensure the firm has a written policy that has been distributed to all employees. Further, they should make sure it contains a statement about the possession and use of drugs and/or alcohol being prohibited on company time and premises, as well as, the actions taken against violators. To enforce compliance, employers may educate the employees on the dangers of on-the-job drug usage and have information available on counseling or rehabilitation.

Copyright © Mometrix Media. You have been licensed one copy of this document for personal use only. Any other reproduction or redistribution is strictly prohibited. All rights reserved.

The Drug-Free Workplace Act of 1988 stipulates that an employer securing a government contract of $25,000 or greater must have a written plan for a drug-free workplace and certify that their establishment is, in fact, drug-free.

Auditors should ensure the organization has policies on hiring and accommodating individuals with disabilities in order to comply with the Americans with Disabilities Act (ADA) of 1990, which makes discrimination against individuals with disabilities unlawful. More specifically, he should verify the following:

The firm's employment application should not have any questions regarding prior illnesses, physical limitations, or previous workers' compensation claims.

Interview questions, hiring standards, and tests must be strictly related to the job. A pre-employment medical exam should not assess the severity of the applicant's disability but rather just assess the applicant's ability to do job functions. The company should honor a request made by an individual with a disability, which is defined as a physical or mental impairment significantly limiting a major life activity, for a reasonable accommodation to help the individual's job performance.

The Equal Employment Opportunity Commission (EEOC) enforces the ADA through informal questionnaires, investigative meetings, settlements, or in federal court. Claims may result in reinstating the employee or offering back pay among other resolutions.

Auditors must evaluate the firm's sexual harassment policy for adequacy. According to the Civil Rights Act of 1991, companies may be held liable for their employees' actions of on-the-job sexual harassment, regardless of whether they are aware of such actions. A victim of sexual harassment includes an employee who loses a promotion to someone who accepted the sexual advances, as well as, an employee receiving inappropriate comments, gestures, and unwanted touching. The determinants of whether a company is liable or to what degree include:

- Whether the company had a comprehensive sexual harassment policy in existence at the time of the incident.
- If the employer responded appropriately and promptly to the claim.
- If a firm is held liable, punitive and compensatory damages may be as high as $300,000.

Legal Obligations

Employers have legal obligations concerning its employees. For example, minimum wages and requirements for overtime pay are mandated by federal and state laws. Additionally, laws require contributions to be made for unemployment insurance and for income tax to be withheld from employee compensation. Under workers' compensation laws, employers must have insurance coverage for employees. Both, independent contractors and employees, complete tasks for a firm in exchange for compensation, yet the employer has the above mentioned responsibilities to only its employees, not contractors. Thus, it's important to distinguish the two. Typically, an independent contractor is an individual who runs his own business doing services for other businesses for a profit, using his own office, tools, and equipment. He decides how to accomplish the project and is paid by the job. An employee works only for the employer, usually at the employer's facility. He works under the direction of his employer, regarding work methods and hours. He is compensated with hourly wages or a salary.

Copyright © Mometrix Media. You have been licensed one copy of this document for personal use only. Any other reproduction or redistribution is strictly prohibited. All rights reserved.

Business Process Reengineering

Business process reengineering (BPR) is a technique that reviews the firm's purpose and goals, and the demands of its customers as a basis for determining more proficient ways of using the firm's resources to meet those demands. BPR involves revamping an organization's overall process. Changes of such magnitude may take years to implement, but the eventual benefits include being able to offer products and/or services at reduced costs, with better quality, and with faster production or service results.

If the overall process already seems efficient or the firm is not in a position to implement major changes, the firm may still benefit from a business process improvement (BPI). A BPI focuses on making incremental changes to specific areas or tasks. Such small changes will not bring the dramatic improvements of a BPR, but they are easier and faster to implement and do bring about some improvement.

Follow-Up Audit Procedures

Once audit observations and suggested recommendations are reported to the appropriate management level, meaning those with the authority to take corrective actions, follow-up procedures, as defined in the internal audit department's charter, should commence. It is the chief audit executive's (CAE's) responsibility to establish these procedures. They should include: a suggested time frame for allowing management to respond to the audit observations and recommendations; evaluation of the timeliness, adequacy, and appropriateness of management's response; scheduling a follow-up meeting; and communicating inappropriate responses or corrective actions to senior management or the board. Factors, such as the significance of the reported finding; the level of risk it poses to the organization; and the costs, resources, time, and complexity for implementing the proposed corrective actions, should be considered to adjust follow-up procedures accordingly.

Copyright © Mometrix Media. You have been licensed one copy of this document for personal use only. Any other reproduction or redistribution is strictly prohibited. All rights reserved.

Perform Other Internal Audit Roles and Responsibilities

Risk Management

Process

First, the internal auditor must determine the organization's objectives and level of risk tolerance, which may be accomplished by speaking to audit committee members, or browsing through their meeting minutes, and reviewing company policies. Next, interviewing management gathers information about the individual area's objectives, risks, and management methodology for minimizing and controlling those risks. To determine if those methods are the most efficient, the auditor must research reference resources and current industry trends to determine the best practices for that particular industry. Evaluating thoroughness of the risk management process requires studying management's risk analysis, reviewing prior risk evaluations, including those from other sources, and observing if prior concerns were dealt with adequately. His final assessment is based on whether the area's business strategies agree with the company's objectives and whether the amount and types of risk assumed by management do not exceed the company's level of risk tolerance. Also, it is based on the efficiency of management's methods of controlling risk and the adequacy of the process.

Members Responsible

Upper management designs and maintains risk management and control processes to protect company assets, monitor the accuracy of information reported, reach peak operational efficiency, and ensures practices abide with legal requirements. Upper and operational management are responsible for assessing their unit's controls. The internal audit department is to formulate an overall opinion of the organization's control system based on various areas assessed. Those areas are based on the CAE's audit plan, as he must include all business functions, areas of major or changing operations, and those with high risk. To avoid duplication, the plan should incorporate using managerial assessments and external audit reports. The amount and severity of weaknesses found, and how they were dealt with would be considered and used to support his decision on whether the organization's risks are controlled to an acceptable level. The CAE reports annually about the effectiveness of the organizations' risk management and control processes to upper management and the board.

Assessments

Risk management assessment extends to environmental, health, and safety (EH&S) risks. These types of risk include costs for meeting new Environmental Protection Agency (EPA) requirements, the firm's potential for harming the environment and getting sued or fined, and also drastic drops in customer consumption of the firm's products or services due to a negative public image. Some organizations have the CAE assume responsibility for environmental auditing. However, most organizations separate the environmental audit function, led by an environmental audit chief, from the internal audit department. In some organizations, the CAE and the environmental audit chief coordinate their efforts. Within other organizations they have little interaction.

Absence of Process

One of the internal auditor's responsibilities is assessing and improving the effectiveness of risk management. It is possible, though, that an organization has yet to create a risk management process. In this situation, an internal auditor must discuss, with management, the importance of developing one and may provide them with a few suggestions. However, the extent of the auditor's involvement with creating a risk management process should be determined by management and

Copyright © Mometrix Media. You have been licensed one copy of this document for personal use only. Any other reproduction or redistribution is strictly prohibited. All rights reserved.

the board. If they do ask for his assistance, he would be providing consulting services and the internal audit department's charter would have to reflect his role in the risk management process.

Enterprise Risk Management

For years, risk management has narrowed its attention to the financial and hazard risks that could affect an organization. Financial risks have to do with fluctuations in the market. For example, if interest rates rise, the cost of borrowing money for obtaining necessary assets also rises; and if the company's stock value drops, it receives less capital per share. Hazard risks are those associated with natural disasters, or other types of property damage, or certain employee liabilities, all of which are insurable.

Enterprise risk management (ERM) broadens its focus to not only address financial and hazard risks but also strategic and operational risks. Strategic risks deal with high-level situations, such as risks associated with compliance, key employees, reputation, and marketing. Operational risks deal with the components that could affect day-to-day business operations, such as technology, employees, and processes. By addressing more types of risks, management strives to increase shareholder value, not just protect it.

Categorizing Risk

Risk may be categorized as subjective or objective, static or dynamic, and pure or speculative.

Risk that is subjective means it is based on a person's doubts or worries, as opposed to objective reasoning that is more identifiable and measurable.

Static risk refers to risks that may occur in a stable environment, such as lightning striking in our everyday world. Dynamic risk refers to risk occurring in a changing environment, such as constant changes in legislature.

Pure risk refers to incidents that result in a loss or no loss. Speculative risk refers to incidents that result in a profit or loss.

Risk Financing

Risk financing refers to the methods and costs for either internally assuming a risk or externally transferring it. Internally assuming the risk may either ye unfunded, thus a residual risk, or funded by reserving funds, self-insuring, or using credit.

Risk transfer is when the party with the risk pays another party to assume the risk. The various types of risk transfer include: hold-harmless agreements, diversification, hedging, incorporation, and insurance.

Transferring Risk

Companies may form a captive insurance company. The captive will issue an insurance policy to its parent and charge premiums. This is a form of risk transfer because the company is transferring the risk to the captive, as well as, risk retention because the company owns the captive.

Multiline/Multiyear insurance contracts allow unrelated risks to be combined into a single policy over multiple years. An example of coverage for this type of contract would be $10,000 per incident, $20,000 per year, and $50,000 for the life of the contract. Financial insurance contracts are used to defer risk over time.

Copyright © Mometrix Media. You have been licensed one copy of this document for personal use only. Any other reproduction or redistribution is strictly prohibited. All rights reserved.

Multiple trigger policies are used when a company may handle one adverse event at a time, but not multiple unrelated adverse events at the same time. These policies cover the bundle of unrelated risks at relatively lower premiums but only pay claims when all of the risks named in the policy occur.

Securitization is the packaging of risks into securities as a form of insurance. The risk is transferred to the investor. For example, earthquake bonds may be issued by a company who wants to protect itself from an earthquake. Investors buy the bonds and the company pays them interest. If no earthquake occurs, the company pays back the principal when the bond matures. If an earthquake does occur, the company does not pay back the principal but uses the money to cover its losses.

Internal Control Guidance

Management and internal auditors, who may be helping design an internal control system, may refer to the Internal Control – Integrated Framework report published by the Committee of Sponsoring Organizations (COSO) of the Treadway Commission. The IIA recommends using the COSO model for providing an internal controls framework since it is highly-effective and easily applicable. It does not just narrowly focus on the accounting and financial process. It addresses other factors that may also affect financial reporting: asset safeguarding, efficient and effective procedures, and compliance with company policies and legal regulations. However, particular industries or legalities may dictate using other recognized models that would be better suited to their needs.

Control Self-Assessment

A control self-assessment (CSA), also known as a control/risk self-assessment (CRSA), is a formal structured method for evaluating risk management and control processes. Management and employees identify risks in their area, assess the current control processes, produce risk-reduction plans, and verify their ability of still accomplishing business objectives.

The advantage to this methodology is the involvement of more people learning and becoming aware of risks in their areas and the necessity of minimizing those risks through controls. Feeling more involved, employees tend to respond quicker and more effectively when corrective actions must be implemented. Also, control is being self-assessed throughout the company, freeing more time for the internal audit's efforts to focus on areas with high-risk or greater weaknesses.

Control self-assessment (CSA) programs are unique to each organization, customized to fit a firm's philosophies and business dynamics. However, three basic methods have emerged: team workshops, surveys, and management-produced analysis.

Team workshops are comprised of a leader and a team of employees, representing various levels in a function. Information is gathered from discussions about objectives, risks, and controls and put into a report. The team may vote on different ideas and thoughts in the report, either openly or anonymously. Surveys are typically objective questions about risks and controls in the area. This style of CSA may be favored by areas with a large employee base or by management who feels this approach is more cost-effective. Management-produced analysis is management's own approach to determining its risk and the effectiveness of its controls. This is typically used as a quick assessment of something particular in a control process.

Audit Department's Involvement

Since a CSA program provides company-wide assessments of control processes and encourages better responses to recommended corrective actions, it is to the advantage of the internal audit

- 42 -

Copyright © Mometrix Media. You have been licensed one copy of this document for personal use only. Any other reproduction or redistribution is strictly prohibited. All rights reserved.

department to help design, implement and maintain a CSA program by providing training, workshop facilitators, and guidance as needed. At a minimum, the internal audit department should serve as an advisor for the program and verify the self-assessments. In this instance, management may use such control models as the COSO (Committee of Sponsoring Organizations) of the Treadway Commission and CoCo (Criteria of Control) for training purposes, workshop guidance, and to verify the thoroughness of the assessment.

Environmental Audits

Categories of environmental audits recognized by the IIA include:

- Compliance audits – This is the most common type of environmental audit. Its objective is to assess whether the activities and operations are carried out in accordance with applicable laws and regulations. Before the actual compliance audit, a preliminary assessment, also known as a document review or desktop audit, is done to identify possible problem areas.
- Environmental Management System audits – These assess the organization's control policies and procedures, which are designed to protect the environment and to manage future environmental risks.
- Acquisition and Divestiture audits – The purpose is to evaluate the environmental risks associated with property that is to be acquired or used as collateral. They are also known as property transfer evaluations, transactional audits, or due diligence audits.
- Treatment, Storage, and Disposal Facility audits – These assess whether the government's environmental regulations for hazardous materials are followed. These regulations stipulate that hazardous materials must be properly tracked from their creation to their disposal, with owners being liable for them throughout.
- Pollution Prevention audits – These are typically done in manufacturing firms. They study and evaluate operations for the purpose of identifying sources of waste and/or pollution and offering corrective suggestions.
- Environmental Liability Accrual audits – These are usually done by the internal audit function. They are to evaluate whether the estimated costs for fixing known environmental issues are reasonable and are properly accounted and reported.
- Product audits – These take place in the production department and are for the purpose of evaluating whether the product complies with chemical restrictions and other environmental concerns, such as the ability to be recycled.

Environmental Strategy

Environmental audits may be comprehensive or have a limited audit scope, focusing on a particular area, such as the organization's environmental strategy, environmental issues within a firm's functions, or ecological concerns in operations.

Audit procedures for reviewing an organization's environmental strategy are as follows:

- Determine whether a general environmental policy exists; if it has been distributed to employees, shareholders, customers, suppliers, and regulatory authorities, such as the EPA; and whether it is supported by the board of directors, upper management, and the employees.
- Review methods for implementing changes that are designed to improve environmental performance and the procedures for evaluating them.

Copyright © Mometrix Media. You have been licensed one copy of this document for personal use only. Any other reproduction or redistribution is strictly prohibited. All rights reserved.

- Assess the training and motivation offered to employees for learning, developing, and following new environmentally-conscious practices.
- Verify the existence of written procedures to follow in the event of an environmental accident or emergency, including the role of public relations.

Risks and Results

When assessing a firm's environmental risks, auditors should make a list of all potential environmental concerns and rank them as high, moderate, or low risk. Those with the highest risk of threatening the firm's long-term existence should be audited first and have the highest priority for receiving funds to make changes that alleviate those risks. Such expenditures should be audited to assess whether they were used effectively, resulting in greater control of the company's environmental risk.

The results of an environmental audit should be reported in summary to the board of directors, along with recommendations. The recommendations should include the resources, estimated cost, and approximate time needed to implement the changes, as well as, a suggested date for the next review. The auditor should seek board approval for the recommendations and schedule deadlines for their implementation. Any significant deficiencies found during the audit should be reported immediately to the chief audit executive (CAE).

Business Functions

Audit procedures for an environmental audit are as follows for these business functions:

- Marketing function
- Determine if marketing strategies include advertising the product's environmentally superior features, as well as, creating an image of being an environmentally conscious company.
- Assess whether the product packaging is environmentally friendly (i.e., biodegradable, recyclable)
- Finance function
- Evaluate whether investment decisions consider and address environmental concerns, including looking for other environmental-friendly alternatives, even if they are more costly.
- Legal function
- Ensure all legal requirements for adhering to environmental regulations are met.
- Determine if all liability risks for environmental damage are minimized.
- Production function
- Inquire whether acquiring new facilities or improved, nonpolluting machinery has been considered.
- Determine if ecological materials are used.
- Analyze the methods used to minimize emissions.
- Evaluate whether raw materials are efficiently used, with minimal wastage.
- Insurance function
- Confirm that environmental risks have been analyzed to determine their potential damage, including indirect effects to third parties.
- Assess the adequacy of risk management's plans for assuming, insuring, and transferring environmental risks.

- 44 -

Copyright © Mometrix Media. You have been licensed one copy of this document for personal use only. Any other reproduction or redistribution is strictly prohibited. All rights reserved.

Ecological Concerns

Environmental audit procedures & ecological concern addressed:

- Assess the adequacy of controls over the discharges of air, water, and noise to ensure they comply with laws and regulations. Discharges- Determine whether energy-conservation methods have been implemented.
- Energy Usage - Inquire whether alternative energy sources, such as solar or wind energy, have been considered.
- Energy Usage- Assess methods for reducing water consumption, such as controlling leaks or finding alternative cooling methods.
- Water Usage- Make sure recyclable and non-recyclable waste is segregated and both are disposed accordingly.
- Waste and Recycling- Determine if recyclable supply products are bought, used, and recycled. Ensure litter is eliminated and grounds are maintained. Pollution- Determine if environmentally-conscious means are used for the transport of raw materials, products, and staff. Evaluate methods for encouraging public transportation or car-pooling. Make sure company cars are low-pollution models.

Team Workshops

Objective-Focused

A workshop with an objective focus concentrates on the need to meet business goals. First, they consider current control procedures and how they support the objectives. Next, they evaluate what risks still remain, known as residual risks, and determine if they are small enough to be allowed.

Risk-Focused

A workshop focusing on risk begins with listing all possible obstacles that may be encountered while trying to meet an objective. After singling out the major risk factors, they decide if their controls are adequate for managing those risks.

Control-Focused

A workshop that is focused on controls is designed to analyze the difference between management's expectations of the controls and their actual effectiveness. It begins with the major risks and controls already identified. The team simply assesses the controls' effectiveness in dealing with risks and their supportiveness in meeting objectives.

Process-Focused

A workshop with a process focus goes beyond evaluating controls. It evaluates and tries to improve an entire process, such as product design or development. It begins by considering the objectives of the process and figuring new ways to meet them while factoring in risks and controls.

Certifications in Financial Statements

The U.S. Securities and Exchange Commission (SEC) has particular requirements for reporting quarterly and annual financial statements and specifications for necessary disclosures and certifications. The Sarbanes-Oxley Act of 2002 enacted more stringent requirements on disclosures and certifications. The requirements mandate that both the principal executive officer(s) and the principal financial officer(s) certify that they have reviewed the financial report, and to the best of their knowledge, it is true, accurate, and a fair representation of the company's financial condition with no omissions of material information.

Copyright © Mometrix Media. You have been licensed one copy of this document for personal use only. Any other reproduction or redistribution is strictly prohibited. All rights reserved.

Now they must further certify that they have created and implemented disclosure controls and procedures, which they have evaluated within the past ninety days and have included the results in the report.

Finally, they certify that they disclosed the following information to the auditors and the audit committee: any weaknesses with the internal controls relating to financial reporting, any fraud connected to individuals who partake in the internal control process, and any major changes in the internal control process since the last evaluation.

Compliance

For firms to be able to govern the reporting process of quarterly statements internal auditors should make sure written policies and procedures of the process exist. Also, internal auditors may try to organize a disclosure committee made up of representatives from areas that help contribute input to the reports' disclosures, such as financial managers, the CAE, and legal advisors. The disclosure committee would oversee and guide the process. Finally, internal auditors may validate management's self-assessments or serve as an independent assessor by periodically evaluating the financial reporting and disclosure processes and providing the results and recommendations to management and the audit committee.

Basic Roles

Upper management is accountable for the financial data and disclosures contained in the reports since the input is derived from areas under its control. External auditors test the validity of the financial report to determine if it is an accurate portrayal of the firm's financial condition. This assurance is necessary for financial report users since important decisions may be based on its results. Internal auditors assess the effectiveness of the controls used in the financial reporting and disclosing processes. This assurance is for the benefit of upper management and the audit committee.

Controls

The financial reporting process is the sequence of steps from obtaining the data through to preparing the financial statements with its notes and necessary disclosures. Controls are embedded throughout the process to prevent mistakes, inaccurate estimates or assumptions, and detect unusual activities of recordings. In general, they are designed to ensure that the financial statements are correct and do not mislead or inaccurately portray the firm's financial condition. The CAE is usually asked by the audit committee and executive management to evaluate the internal control processes. Once the committee receives his report, they review it and send their own conclusive report to the board of directors.

Information Technology Providers

Many business transactions involve at least three parties: the purchaser, supplier, and a third-party provider. Third-party providers of information technology may be categorized as: consultants, vendors, system integrators, or service providers. Internal auditors should assess relevant controls in the computer center at the third-party provider's premises. Consultants are typically hired under short-term contracts to accomplish specific jobs, such as analyzing, designing, and improving computer application systems. Vendors of hardware and software assist their clients with hardware installations, software integration, as well as, provide technical support, training, and service agreements. System integrators are outside organizations hired to effectively integrate the firm's multiple software products with its hardware and network configurations.

Copyright © Mometrix Media. You have been licensed one copy of this document for personal use only. Any other reproduction or redistribution is strictly prohibited. All rights reserved.

Service Providers

Service providers are third-party organizations that provide information system (IS) services. The various types of service providers include:

Service bureaus provide information system (IS) services for processing specified applications in exchange for a set fee.

Timesharing facilities also provide IS services but charge by the usage.

Third-party network service providers are organizations that provide a telecommunications network, allowing an exchange of data between user organizations, such as between a buyer and supplier.

Financial service organizations provide businesses with charge card transaction services.

Outsourcing management takes place when an organization hires another organization, typically with a five to six-year contract, to manage and operate its IS area and network services. As management has relinquished control over a function, it is important to monitor the activities of the outsourced function.

Personal Privacy

Protection of personal privacy must be considered by risk management. Its definition extends to the gathering, use, and reporting of personal information. Name, address, credit history, employee files, and evaluations are examples of personal information. Risks associated with an organization's infringement upon someone's rights to privacy include: defamation to each parties' reputations, a mistrusting company environment, and lawsuits. Furthermore, businesses are legally required to have privacy controls. An internal auditor is usually asked to determine what information is considered personal and if the collection of that information is acceptable. Also, he may be asked to provide assurance that the method of gathering and the use of the information adheres to legal standards. During an internal auditor's evaluation of an organization's privacy controls, he may work with an in-house legal advisor for interpretation of privacy laws and regulations. He may also need an information technology specialist to validate the existence of data security controls.

Privacy Audit Engagements

Privacy audit engagements focus on privacy issues. Privacy refers to an individual's right to have personal information kept confidential. Internal auditors ensure data is properly collected and used, as well as, assess current controls used to safeguard against accidental or deliberate disclosure of employees' personal or a corporation's proprietary records. Nearly all privacy laws require firms to implement controls to protect confidential information. Since most confidential information is in computer files; internal auditors must ensure the system has adequate controls, such as passwords, user IDs, encryption, hidden files, and pop-up warnings, to minimize assessed risks and exposures. Auditors routinely monitor the efficiency and effectiveness of these controls. In addition, internal auditors must also make sure there is proof of compliance in the event of a court case. An accessible, updated manual with documentation of the policies that address privacy and the handling of violations, standard operating procedures, controls, and applicable laws and regulations would be proof.

Copyright © Mometrix Media. You have been licensed one copy of this document for personal use only. Any other reproduction or redistribution is strictly prohibited. All rights reserved.

Information Security

The safeguarding of vital company information is management's responsibility. In order to provide assurance of the adequacy and effectiveness of the information security controls, the Chief Audit Executive (CAE) must make sure the audit department has the necessary resources for performing this type of evaluation. Management must inform the auditors of any security breaches or incidents during the assessment. Examples of security controls may include access authorizations, protective software, or physical security of data storage servers. The internal auditor must periodically evaluate how effective the controls are at preventing or detecting information theft, loss, or misuse. His report should contain improvement recommendations or suggestions for new controls, as necessary.

Security Audits

Types of security audits and their respective audit scopes are as follows:

Physical security audits inspect physical access to areas with valuable assets, such as inventory warehouses, or with sensitive information, such as computer centers and research laboratories. The types of controls that would be evaluated in such an audit would be access controls (i.e., electronic card access, voice recognition devices) and natural disaster controls (i.e., fire extinguishing sprinkler system, insurance policies).

Logical security audits address computer system access authorizations and require testing of user ID codes, passwords, and reviewing encryption methods.

Computer storage media audits assess the availability of storage capacity, study the movement of computer files to and from off-site storage, and review environmental controls.

Safety audits inspect the safety policies and procedures; review accident reports, checking that proper corrective actions were taken; and ensure the organization is in compliance with labor laws. Safety audits often require coordination with other auditing efforts in the following functions: quality, health, security, and industrial engineering.

Power Surges and Outages

Computer equipment does not work during brownouts or blackouts and may be damaged by power surges or spikes. Therefore, auditors must assess the environmental controls that safeguard the computer center from power surges and outages. For example, he may ensure the risk of voltage surges and sags is minimized by verifying the computer power source does not share its power supply with other major electrical sources, such as the air conditioning and heating units which may cause voltage fluctuations as they turn on and off. An auditor must determine if the local power supply is reliable, or if it is necessary to use an uninterruptible power supply (UPS) machine, with a generator backup.

Copyright © Mometrix Media. You have been licensed one copy of this document for personal use only. Any other reproduction or redistribution is strictly prohibited. All rights reserved.

Security of Software

Through reviewing, testing, and interviewing head operating system personnel, such as the systems programming manager or technical services manager, an auditor may assess the security of operating systems software by:

- Ensuring passwords are used to restrict system programmers from accessing system areas that do not pertain to their current job tasks.
- Using a program comparator tool to determine if security is adequate in preventing unauthorized changes to the operating system software. The tool allows the auditor to compare total bit counts at different points in time; an unequal count is evidence that changes have been made to the software.
- Comparing bit counts or hash totals of records allows the auditor to discover breaches in security of the internal tables.
- Ensuring the system's data files are protected from unauthorized browsing or scavenging by making sure the operating system has a feature to erase a job's scratch space once a job is terminated.
- Checking for tight controls over commands that inactivate the logging activities within the operating system.

Performance-Gauging Tools

An auditor should review the following operating systems software's performance-gauging tools:

- Analysis of disk input/output (I/O) activity across volumes – This shows ideal data set placement across volumes for balancing strings to minimize path contention and reduce queue time.
- Evaluation of the effective use of the cache resource – This determines which volumes or data sets belong under cache based on the cache model and storage size.
- Recommendations for data set reorganization – These recommendations are based on analyses of the directory access and data set members.
- Data reorganization simulation – This calculates the percentage of improved efficiency in the event of company reorganization.
- History files – These are necessary for doing trend analyses.
- I/O volume reports – These are available by job, data set, or unit.
- Exception reports – When too many jobs are competing for the same volume's resources, this report indicates which jobs are involved.

Application System

Auditors are often asked to help in the development of an application system to ensure adequate controls are built into it. Their input in the early phases of development with regard to system requirements, security control requirements, and software testing methods and schedules may save time and money by guiding the system designers in a direction that will not require major changes or added controls in the future.

Another critical phase when it is best to have auditor participation is during file/system conversion and after implementation, as it is crucial to have system reviews during this phase. It is important to note, auditors' duties do not include designing or installing computer application systems, but rather reviewing, testing, and evaluating application systems based on IT/IS standards.

Copyright © Mometrix Media. You have been licensed one copy of this document for personal use only. Any other reproduction or redistribution is strictly prohibited. All rights reserved.

Auditor Participation

The amount of auditor participation depends on the audit staff's available time and skill levels, as well as, the risk level of the system under development. There are four possible ways to participate. The two proactive approaches are for the auditor to have continuous involvement or to help during the critical stages of development, such as system requirements planning, testing, and conversion. Since these approaches have the auditor's input during the development, stronger control designs may be created, reducing the need for controls to be reworked in the future. This, however, requires more auditor time and effort, and thus increases audit costs. The other two approaches are reactive, as the auditor's participation is either after the entire system is implemented or at the end of critical stages. While these approaches reduce audit cost, the resulting control design may be less effective and require work to be redone, which may result in higher expenses.

Software Development

The software development, acquisition, and maintenance methodology provides the procedures and standards for IT/IS staff and system users to follow. It incorporates management's philosophy as it explains the stages necessary for completing software development, acquisition, and maintenance projects. The required and optional tasks and expected deliverables, or end products, of each stage should be included. The methodology should explain the responsibilities of the IT staff and the functional department users. It should provide the criteria for controls, security, and audit trails, as well as, for software quality, usability, and maintainability. And finally, it provides guidance on the use of tools and techniques of software development, conversion, and maintenance.

Auditors are responsible for auditing computer application systems under development. To determine which projects to audit first, they rank them as high, medium, and low risk; with high-risk projects being audited first. Risk evaluations are based on the following factors: total cost and hours attributed to the project; the nature and scope of the system; the value of the assets it controls; its effect on the financial statements; computer processing mode and programming language being used; total number of programs/modules involved; and legal or regulatory requirements imposed.

The first step in auditing a computer application system under development is to review the software development, acquisition, and maintenance methodology, which contains the standards for which the project should be measured against. The auditor must ensure the methodology is complete, understandable, achievable, and consistent with: company policies and procedures, management's philosophy, generally accepted industry and IT/IS standards, and regulatory requirements. Furthermore, he should ascertain that it is updated to reflect hardware/software upgrades, as well as, changes in: business or system strategies, management direction, development and maintenance tools and techniques, and control or audit requirements. The next step in the audit process is to review the computer application system under development and test its adherence to the standards provided in the methodology. Deficient findings and recommended corrective actions are to be reported to management. However, the ultimate responsibility for ensuring system users and IT staff members are complying with standards belongs to senior management.

Software Acquisition Process

Auditors work with the software project team as controls specialists and systems consultants. They review the software requirements and use them for evaluating the adequacy of the software's usability, controllability, maintainability, and ability to be audited. They participate in the testing of its tools, functions, and capabilities to determine if it performs according to accompanying

- 50 -

Copyright © Mometrix Media. You have been licensed one copy of this document for personal use only. Any other reproduction or redistribution is strictly prohibited. All rights reserved.

documentation, which is also assessed for adequacy and completeness. They express an opinion as to whether it fulfills the software requirements and may recommend purchasing or not purchasing the selected software package. However, the final purchase decision is made by the functional users' operating management and other appropriate personnel. After the purchase is made, auditors participate in guiding, reviewing, and testing modifications, as well as, the installation of the software. It is important to note purchased software misses the benefits of auditor participation in its development.

<u>Software Attributes</u>

The audit scope of a software development, acquisition, and maintenance audit, would include the following software assessments:

- Usability – Auditors assess the user-friendliness of software and the clarity of its documentation. Response times should be quick; video display unit (VDU/CRT) screen menus should be simple to use; and the system should be flexible for handling unusual circumstances.
- Controllability – Auditors assess an applications system's automated, manual, and compensating controls to ensure data input, processing, and output are accurate and reliable.
- Ability for a Secured Access - Auditors assess the built-in security controls designed to prevent and detect unauthorized access and use of the system's hardware, software, and data.
- Maintainability – Auditors evaluate how easily software may be revised. Software that is designed with structured techniques is easier to modify, creating a more flexible system that may be expanded or adapted to business changes.
- Ability for Auditing – Auditors should review the audit trails that are designed into the system and determine if they provide sufficient data that is reliable and allows the system to be audited according to generally accepted auditing standards (GAAS) or generally accepted government auditing standards (GAGAS).

<u>Data Communications Software</u>

Data communications software supports online application systems by providing the interfaces between the online application systems and the operating systems. This is done through its control program modules; each module has its own specific function, such as transmitting terminal messages or loading programs for transaction processing. Review of the data communications within a network environment requires a high-level of technical understanding. Therefore, a technical advisor may need to assist the auditor. Audit objectives include assessing controls over data communications software and its messages by:

- Reviewing message destinations to ensure they are authorized locations in the network.
- Verifying input/output messages have sequence numbers and are logged, along with, the user's password and terminal ID.
- Ensuring phone numbers for incoming dial-up connections are confidential and changed periodically.

Local Area Network Administrator

In order for an auditor to ensure the LAN administrator is fulfilling his duties, it is important for the auditor to know what those duties include. A local area network (LAN) administrator is responsible for overseeing the operation of a LAN, including its servers and connected destinations.

Copyright © Mometrix Media. You have been licensed one copy of this document for personal use only. Any other reproduction or redistribution is strictly prohibited. All rights reserved.

For security reasons, a LAN administrator should be the only person who may add or delete server names, as well as, set the server's parameters, such as and the maximum number of concurrent users, volumes, printers, and open files per server and the maximum server volume size. His duties also include monitoring the network's performance and identifying problems, which may be achieved with the use of network monitoring software or protocol analyzers.

Computer Contingency Plans

As a member of the disaster recovery/computer contingency planning team, the auditor advises the team on what should be included in the plans. He attends problem-solving meetings, reviews drafted plans, assesses proposed recovery sites, and participates in testing the plan and making recommendations. He ensures there are procedures in place for monitoring and maintaining the computer contingency plans, such as requiring functional users to maintain backup computer centers with updated data files and current versions of application programs and of the operating system. Another important duty is for the auditor to assess if insurance coverage of the IT resources (i.e., computer hardware, software, and data) is adequate.

The computer contingency plans should be understandable and complete. To be complete, they should, at minimum, include such things as: names, addresses, and phone numbers of the recovery team members, emergency team instructions, arrangements for a temporary work location in the event of a disaster, identity of computer equipment suppliers, a diagram and description of an emergency network configuration, instructions for redirecting incoming calls to connect with the recovery site, and alternate communication plans in case of failed phone lines (i.e., cable or microwave satellite links).

Storing Records Off-Site

If the computer contingency plans require computer, paper, and microfilm records to be stored off-site by a third party, the auditor should investigate that party's financial position, reputation, and adherence to storage standards. It is also important to find out whether they have media replacement insurance, protecting the media from negligent loss, misplacement, or damage. The auditor should visit the storage facility to evaluate the adequacy of its physical security, fire prevention, and environmental controls. He should inquire whether they have a log, tracking the movement of media between sites, and determine whether it is detailed enough to locate media in case it becomes misplaced.

Database System's Performance

A database has a data storage unit connected to a memory unit. The storage unit transfers a data file to the memory unit for it to temporarily hold while a user is accessing and using the file. To improve the database system's performance, the auditor may suggest increasing its memory, adding data storage units, or reorganizing the database. When the database is reorganized, the auditor should make sure the DBA compares the control totals before and after the reorganization to confirm that they match, ensuring the integrity of the data files. The system's response time may be improved by distributing the work load so that peak times are smoothed out, maintaining more consistent usage among fewer employees at a time. An auditor may also evaluate the costs/benefits of acquiring data compression software which compresses huge volumes of database records, thereby allowing more data storage per disk. Costs are reduced since fewer disks are needed, and backup processing is faster.

- 52 -

Copyright © Mometrix Media. You have been licensed one copy of this document for personal use only. Any other reproduction or redistribution is strictly prohibited. All rights reserved.

Preventing Computer Viruses

An auditor may ensure an organization has adequate controls for preventing computer viruses by:

- Ensuring the LAN administrator or data security administrator remove inactive user accounts from the network files and directories, as well as, unlicensed programs from PCs and network files.
- Assessing the use of logical controls, such as requiring passwords, allowing only restricted access to files and directories, and blocking "write" commands on tapes and diskettes, to minimize virus risk.
- Determining if controls to prevent hackers from penetrating the system are used. For example, passwords should be encrypted when they are sent over the wire and dial-back modems should be used when network access is obtained by dial-in.
- Evaluating the adequacy of antiviral software and of programs designed to sweep the system to detect the following changes within a file: size, date and content.
- Making sure all new and modified software, whether it's internally developed or purchased from a vendor, should be tested in a test environment to ensure it is virus-free.
- Determining if system users are aware of how to adequately prevent and detect computer viruses, including doing daily comparisons of executable program files and taking note of any inexplicable changes, which may be virus-related.
- Making sure system backups are regularly made, and contingency/recovery plans include procedures for virus attacks.

Electronic Mail

While auditing the electronic mail system, the objective is to assess the policies and controls governing the system to determine if they are adequate. Procedures include:

- Determining if a user ID and password is required to gain access to the system. The system should periodically instruct the user to change his password.
- Reviewing a sample of e-mail messages to ensure employees are using the system for business purposes only.
- Determining if the allowable length of time for e-mail documents to stay on the system before being purged is reasonable.
- Making sure employees are not sending too large of e-mail documents.
- Ensuring access to e-mail does not automatically allow access to other systems, such as business application and database systems, as they should have their own access requirements.

Encryption Methods

Auditors should determine if the organization is effectively using encryption methods to protect sensitive corporate information and its employees' personal records. They may do this by reviewing the encryption methods and assessing their level of protection based on their key lengths. A longer key provides more protection. Also, the auditor should assess the controls and procedures for issuing and distributing digital signatures or certificates.

The objective of auditing enterprise-wide resource planning (ERP) system software is to verify it is achieving strategic and operational goals. The auditor should review management's reasoning for acquiring the ERP system and their expectations from its use. The auditor should determine how

Copyright © Mometrix Media. You have been licensed one copy of this document for personal use only. Any other reproduction or redistribution is strictly prohibited. All rights reserved.

well the ERP system has integrated with the other application systems and whether it has increased the efficiency of internal work flow processes, lowered costs, or improved revenues.

Hazard Communication Standards

Improper handling of hazardous chemicals may cause explosions, fires, bodily injury or harm, or water and sewage contamination. To protect the millions of workers handling hazardous chemicals, the Occupational Safety and Health Administration (OSHA) has issued Hazard Communication Standards, which require manufacturers and distributors to make employers aware of the hazards associated with the chemicals they use. Employers are responsible for passing on this information to their employees. Auditors must ensure their organization complies with these Hazard Communication Standards:

- Create a written Hazard Communication Program
- Using Safety Data Sheets (SDS), identify and document chemical hazards and the precautions used for their handling
- Affix warning labels on hazardous chemical containers
- Teach employees about chemical hazards and the importance for safety procedures and equipment.
- Make available requested information (including limited trade secrets) to health care professionals treating an employee who has been exposed to chemicals.

Computer Crime

Subjects of a computer crime may be past or current employees or outsiders, such as hackers, phrackers, crackers, virus writers, or cloners. Objects used in the crime may include networks, computers, processes, switches, programs, and data. There are various possible targets for an attack. Those that disrupt service include:

- Overloading the hard disk, making it inoperable
- Overloading the bandwidth to "tie up" the network
- Blocking the cache
- Using up all the swap space, disallowing others to use it
- Misallocating large amounts of random access memory (RAM), taking it from places that need it and putting it in areas that don't need it
- Overloading the kernel tables to create system disasters

Computer Forensics

Computer forensics is about capturing computer data in a way that allows it to be admissible evidence in court, thereby increasing the chances of convicting the computer criminal. Forensic tools may include: audit software and tools, virus protection software, utility programs, disk imaging software, password cracking software, cable testers, and line monitors. Examples of good computer forensics include: immediately cutting network links to a computer system that is believed to be used in a crime; leaving evidence untouched while capturing it; using time/date stamps as proof of when transactions occurred; protecting evidence, whether it's hardware, programs, or data, from being tampered with or fabricated; and storing electronic evidence on tape or CD-ROM so it's easy to protect and present in court while being difficult for others to dispute its existence.

- 54 -

Copyright © Mometrix Media. You have been licensed one copy of this document for personal use only. Any other reproduction or redistribution is strictly prohibited. All rights reserved.

Computer Hash Codes

Computer hash codes allow computer forensics to quickly locate software that has been tainted. This is how it works. The secure hash algorithm (SHA-1) is a program that computes a hash code for each file. A new hash code is assigned to the file each time one bit or more of the file is changed. Other hash values computed for each file are the message digest 4 (MD4), message digest 5(MD5), and a 32-bit cyclic redundancy checksum (CRC32). All of these hash codes create a set of "fingerprints" for each file which may be compared to the standard "fingerprints" stored in the National Software Reference Library's (NSRL's) reference data set (RDS) database. This reference library was created by the National Institute of Standards and Technology and contains all known program executable files, word processors, network browsers, library files, operating system files, and many others. Files under investigation that do not have matching "fingerprints" with those located in the RDS database, should be inspected further, as the mismatch indicates the file has been modified. Also, running comparisons may bring attention to files that should be present but have been deleted, possibly to conceal illegal activities.

Techniques

The "delay" technique is used during computer system attacks. The idea is to delay the criminal long enough for authorities to be able to trace his origin.

The "trap and trace" technique requires the telephone company's involvement in finding the perpetrator by putting traps on in-circuit emulators, network protocol analyzers, and hardware analyzers. In order to legally access the evidence this way and use it in court, a search warrant or court order must be obtained first. Search warrants and court orders are only granted if probable cause of a suspect committing a crime has been established.

Computer Crime Scene

When a crime within an organization involves the use of computer equipment, the workstation and equipment (the crime scene) should be recorded with videotape and/or photographs. This should include the backside of the computer, which shows cable connections.

An investigator must recognize all possible sources of evidence. Nowadays, that often includes computer storage. All storage media should be seized, as deleted files may still be retrievable because the "delete" command does not actually remove the data, but simply allows the disk sectors to be written over.

Computer Evidence

When collecting evidence, paper documents should be handled with cloth gloves and sealed in an evidence container. Computer evidence, such as tapes and disks, should be removed and write-protected immediately to prevent tampering. Appropriate evidence containers should be used; magnetic media, for example, should not be placed in plastic envelopes because an electrical static discharge could damage the evidence. Internal hard-drives should not be removed from the computer, but the read/write heads should be secured with the appropriate software command. Computer cables and ports should be labeled, and the hardware wrapped in plastic. And finally, printer switch settings should be recorded, and the ribbon removed.

Business Attacks

Employee sabotage is when a disgruntled employee tries to harm his company. It is the most common business attack. Examples of employee sabotage by use of a computer include "crashing" computer systems and destroying programs or data. Data diddling is the corruption of computer

Copyright © Mometrix Media. You have been licensed one copy of this document for personal use only. Any other reproduction or redistribution is strictly prohibited. All rights reserved.

data at any stage (input, processing, or output). The most common computer fraud, however, is manipulation of input. Examples include replacing computer tapes with altered ones and entering incorrect data into a program. Superzapping involves the unauthorized use of a computer utility program, which can bypass both operating system controls and access controls, in order to copy, corrupt, delete, add, or deny access to stored data. Comparing current and previous data files can detect superzapping.

Copyright © Mometrix Media. You have been licensed one copy of this document for personal use only. Any other reproduction or redistribution is strictly prohibited. All rights reserved.

Governance, Risk, and Control Knowledge Elements

Cadbury Report of the United Kingdom

According to the Cadbury Report issued by the United Kingdom's committee of corporate governance, the board of directors has a fiduciary duty to protect company assets, which means detecting, if not preventing, fraud is their obligation. As such, the board of directors is responsible for the internal control system over financial management. The directors are required to claim responsibility of the internal control system and report its effectiveness in a statement on financial reports. Internal auditors are responsible for monitoring controls and procedures, and performing fraud investigations for the audit committee. External auditors test and evaluate the validity of the financial reports.

Turnbull and King Model

The Turnbull model from the U.K. refers to a combined code for corporate governance created in 1998 by the London Stock Exchange. This code mandates that directors must review the effectiveness of their company's financial, operational, and compliance controls on a yearly basis and report this action to shareholders. The King Committee on Corporate Governance was established under the Institute of Directors in South Africa. The committee created Code of Corporate Practices and Conduct which it issued in the King Report in 1994. In order for a company to be listed on South Africa's Johannesburg Stock Exchange (JSE), it must comply with this code. In 1998, Germany also created a model that affected company controls with its reforms of corporate governance. This model is known as the KonTraG model.

Structures

Publicly-Held Corporation

The owners of a corporation are the shareholders, and therefore they have control over the enterprise. However, since a corporation has numerous shareholders dispersed around the world it would be impractical for all off the shareholders to be on the company's premises, controlling its operations. Instead, shareholders exercise their control by voting for members to represent the shareholder's interests on the board of directors. The board of directors oversees and directs the management of the company. The management is hired by the board to manage the day-to-day activities, which the employees carry out.

Governance Problems

As the number of shareholders has grown exponentially, shareholders think of themselves as investors rather than owners, creating a separation of ownership from control. Managers are hired as agents of a firm; therefore, they are to act on behalf of the firm's interests. Agency problems exist when a manager makes decisions on his behalf. Corporate laws have allowed management to control the proxy process, giving them an opportunity to influence who gets on the board. This may result in a board that does whatever management wants. Also, many boards contain inside directors. Inside directors have pre-existing connections to the company. Some are senior managers while others may be relatives of the CEO. These connections may inhibit inside directors from having opposing views from the CEO even when it concerns shareholder interest.

Improving Corporate Governance

Changes have taken place among two groups: the board of directors and shareholders. The board of directors is becoming less influenced by management as they reduce the number of inside

Copyright © Mometrix Media. You have been licensed one copy of this document for personal use only. Any other reproduction or redistribution is strictly prohibited. All rights reserved.

directors. They are also creating more committees which assign accountability for the overseeing of certain processes, including the process of governing which is overseen by the governance committee. The National Association of Corporate Directors (NACD) has issued The Governance Committee, a handbook designed to improve the governance process. Shareholders are taking a more active role in governance by forming activist groups, and speaking out at shareholder meetings, and filing lawsuits.

CEO Compensation

Some CEOs have exemplified putting their own interests above the shareholders' with regard to their compensation. While their firms experienced profit losses or employee cut-backs, the CEOs enjoyed salary increases. To support shareholders' concerns, the Securities and Exchange Commission (SEC) adopted stricter disclosure requirements, allowing shareholders to better monitor and to compare a company's financial performance with the CEO's compensation. Also, companies have encouraged CEOs to focus on maintaining or improving their firm's performance by partially compensating them with stock options. Studies show these methods to be working.

Hard and Soft Controls

Hard controls, such as budgets and written authorizations, are objective and easily measured. Operational managers usually employ these types of controls. Evaluating these controls may be accomplished through objective means, as by counting, testing, and using flowcharts. Also managing a business operation requires using hard skills, which are concrete measurable abilities. Problem- targeting, decision-making, solving, and technical skills are deemed hard skills. Soft controls are subjective and not easily measured, such as management philosophies, employee attitudes, communications, and ethical culture. These types of controls are usually put into place by upper management. The skills they must possess to do this are soft skills, which are primarily social skills used for motivating, leading, and communicating. Evaluating soft controls is more subjective and based on others' opinions conveyed through surveys, self-assessments, and interviews.

Internal Control

Internal control is a process woven into business operations to help them achieve the three primary objectives of most organizations: creating and maintaining efficient and effective business operations, producing accurate financial statements, and conducting its business within the legal parameters. It cautions, however, that the control process is affected by people. Unwise judgments in the creation of or changes to the process directed by the board of directors or management, managerial authorization to override the system, human error at the user level, or corruption at any level may contribute faults to the process. Therefore, the control process is not a guarantee that objectives will be met but rather a reasonable assurance.

Assessing Internal Controls

Following the COSO (Committee of Sponsoring Organizations) model helps organizations meet the requirement under the Sarbanes-Oxley Act for including an assessment of the effectiveness of its internal control system and financial reporting procedures in its annual report. The COSO model proposes a tiered auditing approach. First, a company-wide evaluation is accomplished with a self-assessment questionnaire. This is followed by a process-level control evaluation, which focuses on particular processes. Internal auditors perform these assessments through analysis and testing of the controls in a process.

Copyright © Mometrix Media. You have been licensed one copy of this document for personal use only. Any other reproduction or redistribution is strictly prohibited. All rights reserved.

<u>Internal Control Process</u>

According to the COSO framework, the components that form the internal control process are the essential needs for accomplishing the firm's objectives. Each need, or component, is individually necessary for meeting the main objectives of reporting accurate financial statements, operating efficiently and effectively, and following legalities. The first component is the control environment. This is the most basic of necessities: the people and the setting, or environment, in which they work. Next is risk assessment; it is necessary to determine and mange risks within the various functions of the business (i.e., production, sales, marketing, accounting). Naturally control activities must follow; designing control policies and procedures is important for managing risks. Most operational managers implement hard controls while executive management uses soft controls. Information and communication is also imperative to any company. This is needed from the simplest of tasks to the management and control of activities.

<u>Implementing a Particular Control</u>

A decision about implementing a control is often times based on a cost-benefit analysis. This is particularly the case in high-risk areas. Quantifying the cost is relatively straight forward, as opposed to the benefit, which usually requires subjective determinants. Benefits should be viewed from the perspective of what the control, if implemented, would prevent from happening. They must consider what risk the company assumes without the control mechanism and what financial impact that risk could cause. The likelihood of the risk occurring also must be factored into the analysis. Too many controls become expensive and create employee tension. Too few controls would force the firm to assume risks that may endanger its well-being.

Criteria of Control Model

According to the Canadian Institute of Chartered Accountants' CoCo (criteria of control) model, control is defined as "those elements of an organization (including its resources, systems, processes, culture, structure, and tasks) that, taken together, support people in the achievement of the organization's objectives". It further defines an organization's three main objectives as virtually identical to those of the COSO model.

Under this framework, evaluating controls is accomplished using the criteria of twenty items, divided into four groups: purpose, commitment, capability, and monitoring and learning. The criteria may be used for assessing control in various areas of the organization, as they are not specific to internal controls over financial reporting.

Purpose criteria are focused on a company's goals, rules, strategies, risks, and operational progress. Commitment criteria cover organizational and ethical cultures and employee understanding of responsibilities, authority, and accountability. Capability criteria are for assessing competence and communication systems. Monitoring and learning criteria help evaluate the ability to monitor progress, internal/external forces, and procedures for reviewing recommended changes.

Copyright © Mometrix Media. You have been licensed one copy of this document for personal use only. Any other reproduction or redistribution is strictly prohibited. All rights reserved.

Computer Controls

Various classifications of computer controls include:

- Two Main Groups - The broadest classification consists of two groups: general and application controls. General controls are used to maintain all information systems, including mainframes, docking stations, and data output, which cumulatively is the environment needed for application controls to function. Application controls ensure completeness, accuracy, reliability, and proper authorization of the information used in transaction processes. Some may be manual, but most are computerized edit checks built into the software.
- Type - Computer controls may also be categorized based on their type, such as management controls which include policies and procedures, physical controls used to physically secure assets, and logical controls for controlling access into computer files and programs.
- Purpose - Controls may be grouped by their purpose: preventive, detective, corrective, recovery, or directive.
- Function - Functional areas in which the computer controls belong is a final method of categorizing them. Such functional controls may include: development, operations, application, security, network, and user controls.

General Controls

Data center operations controls monitor user processes, job scheduling and initiations (typically automated), as well as, provide backup and recovery mechanisms.

System software controls maintain the use and up-keep of system software, which includes operational, database, security, telecommunications, and utility software. These controls also monitor and log system users.

Access security controls ensure only authorized users have access to restricted files and programs while intercepting intruders. Lists of authorized users should be updated often, and passwords and user IDs of terminated employees should be removed immediately from the system. Application system development controls are used within a system development methodology to control costs and to provide a procedural process for designing, implementing, and documenting each phase. These controls also call for periodic reviews and provide steps to follow to gain approval before making any changes to the system. Sometimes it is less expensive for companies to purchase software packages with customized features than it is to develop application systems themselves.

Review Controls

Tools and techniques for reviewing controls include:

- An audit trail, also known as an information or transaction trail, is the traceable evidence of a transaction from its origination, through its processing, to its final disposal. It shows the sequence of events and the people involved at each stage of the transaction, establishing accountability and discouraging fraud. In addition to auditors, management and government taxing agents also use audit trails for review.
- Control total verification is a technique that uses control totals (i.e., financial totals, quantity totals) to determine if data entry and processing has been performed correctly. For example, accepted totals plus rejected totals (those reported as errors or exceptions) should equal the input totals, as well as, the output totals. Online application systems are able to sort the data and provide control totals based on terminal used, employee entering the data, type of transaction, and location.

- 60 -

Copyright © Mometrix Media. You have been licensed one copy of this document for personal use only. Any other reproduction or redistribution is strictly prohibited. All rights reserved.

- Transaction logs are often used as compensating controls. They contain important system data that auditors use for analyzing and testing. They are also relied upon for recovery from system failures. There are numerous transaction logs, including: console (operating system) log, database log, application transaction log, access control log, telecommunication log, job accounting log, and system management log.
- Error logs document the following information about errors: type of error, when it occurred, employee who fixed it, and when it was fixed. Error summary reports may provide data by error type, person who fixed it, department, division, or application system. An error log is typically found in either or both the IT or system user department.
- Two-dimensional control grids/matrices are created by placing audit risks and security threats on one axis and the controls used to eliminate or minimize those risks on the other axis. This helps illustrate the relationship between risks and controls, allowing an auditor to better evaluate the adequacy and effectiveness of existing controls. This technique is most advantageous to use in continually changing environments.
- Internal control questionnaires (ICQs) have closed-ended, or yes/no, questions regarding internal controls. ICQs help auditors get a general understanding of computer operations or systems and are particularly helpful to inexperienced auditors. Despite their usefulness, however, they do not provide sufficient evidence for evaluating controls and therefore must be supplemented with more in-depth information.
- Exception and statistical reports show data that deviates from allowable standards. Auditors analyze these reports, searching for transaction or operational trends that give rise to such deviations.
- Logical access controls, such as user identification and password codes, keep unauthorized users from accessing restricted computer programs or files. Logical access controls compensate for weak physical access controls.
- Bank reconciliations are a necessary internal control over cash. An employee who is independent from the job duties of receiving or disbursing cash payments and the recording thereof should reconcile monthly bank statements to verify company cash records match the bank account's cash balance. It would be preferable for the employee who reconciles the bank statements to not be from the IT department, as the receiving, disbursing, and recording of cash is done on computer application systems.
- Unannounced independent reviews are used to assess the adequacy of controls over particular systems or procedures. Management may perform such a review if it has concerns about an operation or suspicions about an employee. Alternatively, management may ask auditors or consultants to conduct an independent review of the controls.

Adequacy of Controls

When evaluating the adequacy of controls in an information system (IS), it is necessary to consider the life cycle of the system or process, as controls are interrelated within the phases of a life cycle. A weakness in one phase may affect later phases in the cycle.

The three phases in the life cycle of an application system are: development, operation, and maintenance. Each phase is dominated by different types of controls. For example, project management controls are mostly used in system development; operational controls are designed for system operation; and controls over reconfiguration and program changes are important to system maintenance. Despite the use of different controls in each phase, they are still interrelated within the life cycle, and a weakness in one phase affects the subsequent phases. The same holds true for controls in the life cycle of processes, such as in the data life cycle consisting of the following phases: originating, processing, storing, using, and disposing.

Copyright © Mometrix Media. You have been licensed one copy of this document for personal use only. Any other reproduction or redistribution is strictly prohibited. All rights reserved.

Implementing

Since controls cost money and use resources, careful consideration must be given before deciding to implement a control. Factors to consider include:

- Size of organization and IT department – Smaller organizations or departments may not need as many controls.
- Type of industry and competitive position – A manufacturing company may need more controls than a retail business.
- System or operation's risk levels and management's risk tolerance – Higher risks require more controls while higher-risk tolerance reduces controls needed.
- Value of assets to be safeguarded – The higher the asset value, the greater the risk, and the more controls needed.
- Availability of resources – The greater the resource availability, the more controls an organization can afford.
- Computer technology – The more sophisticated the technology, the more control capabilities it may possess.
- Laws and regulations – The more requirements placed on an organization, the more controls needed.

Electronic Funds Transfer System

A full scope analysis of an electronic funds transfer (EFT) system, typically performed by bank auditors, requires review of the automated teller machine (ATM) systems, automated clearinghouse (ACH) systems, and wire transfer systems. The audit objective in all three areas is to ensure their controls are adequate. Some of the more important controls auditors should review in the ACH and wire transfer systems are as follows:

- ACH Systems
- Processed transactions should be reconciled with the Federal Reserve Bank.
- Rejected items must be adequately handled.
- Wire Transfer Systems
- Methods are used to verify authorization.
- All wire transfers are documented.
- Requests for wires over a predetermined amount must be approved.
- The duties of executing the wire transfer and reconciling due-to, due-from with Federal accounts are segregated.

ATM System

Some of the more important controls governing an ATM system that an auditor should review while auditing an electronic funds transfer system are as follows:

- There should be two employees jointly responsible for the handling, counting, and recording of ATM deposits.
- Most bank employees should be restricted from the computer programs that create customers' personal identification numbers (PINs), as well as, the actual customer PINs.
- ATM cards and PIN mailers should be mailed separately.
- Procedures should be established for handling returned mail, containing ATM cards or PINs, so that employees are prevented from gaining unauthorized access to customer accounts.

Copyright © Mometrix Media. You have been licensed one copy of this document for personal use only. Any other reproduction or redistribution is strictly prohibited. All rights reserved.

- Balancing ATM funds should be done by an employee other than the one who loads and unloads the machine's cash.
- Procedures are followed which adequately control the issuance, processing, and destruction/removal of ATM cards and PINs.

Electronic Data Interchange System

Auditors should review and evaluate the following EDI application controls:

- Audit Trail
- The EDI application puts a time and date stamp on all entered transactions, and it logs the identity of the transaction's operator.
- The system provides before and after images of updated files, and it logs the origin of input transactions, as well as, the destination of output transactions.
- Security
- Access controls and security software are used to protect the EDI application's files, programs, databases, translators, utility programs, and program libraries.
- A security violation within the value-added network (VAN) is automatically logged and further processing is stopped.
- Backup and Recovery
- EDI backup and recovery procedures are tested with the participation of functional users.
- All data and program libraries are routinely backed up.
- Transaction Authorization
- Rejected transactions should be reported and their processing immediately stopped.
- Confirmation notices from transaction originators should be sent automatically, requesting the receiver's acknowledgement.
- Transaction edit controls should prevent the processing of transactions: over predetermined dollar amounts, beyond allowable types of transactions, and by unauthorized parties.
- Transaction Accuracy
- Batch totals are reconciled with transaction input totals to ensure all transactions were entered.
- Transaction errors and rejects are recorded in a queue file, and notification of the error is transmitted to the sender.
- Duplicate transactions are flagged by EDI application controls.
- Data editing controls cannot be overridden or bypassed.
- The EDI has an automatic interface with the payment system to confirm whether the customer has sufficient funds.
- Sensitive transactions cannot be processed without supervisor approval.

Electronic Commerce Processes

The objective of an e-commerce audit is to ensure the processes have effective controls. The procedures for fulfilling that objective include:

- Evaluating the e-commerce software to ensure it provides user-friendly methods for customers to purchase products/services, and it processes transactions in a timely manner.
- Verifying website traffic is monitored to ensure the system can adequately handle the volume.

Copyright © Mometrix Media. You have been licensed one copy of this document for personal use only. Any other reproduction or redistribution is strictly prohibited. All rights reserved.

- Determining if the hardware, server software, server operating system, and value-added network, which is used to create the e-commerce infrastructure, is reliable and secure.
- Assessing the effectiveness of customer authorization controls.
- Making sure the interface between e-commerce and financial systems is reliable.

Master Catalog

To ensure controls over master catalog changes are effective, the auditor should test the adequacy of a small sampling of internal procedures used for controlling master catalog changes. He should verify the existence of effective communications between the data security manager and the technical support group. It is important to review the master catalog changes to confirm that change request forms were completed and that the technical support group did not make changes until the request was approved by the quality control coordinator.

To ensure controls over program systems software changes are effective, the auditor should review a sample of many systems software library changes. He must ensure the change request forms were properly completed and authorized, as well as, assess the evaluation procedures used by the quality control personnel for approving changes before they are installed into the production environment.

Buffer Management System

The performance of batch and online systems may be improved by installing a buffer management system. This system provides more accessible means to storage, which improves batch and online system performance by: reducing the number of input/output (I/O) operations, decreasing the running time of large I/O batch jobs, and cutting back on computer processing unit (CPU) usage. However, installation of the buffer management system may increase paging rates and storage requirements. An auditor must determine if the benefits of a buffer management system outweigh the costs associated with it prior to recommending its installation.

Organizations

There are four main types of organizations: business, nonprofit service, mutual-benefit, and commonweal. Business organizations are in business for the purpose of providing products and/or services to meet the needs of consumers for the ultimate goal of obtaining profits. Nonprofit service organizations' goal is to provide a service. Since they are not operating for a profit and have limited funds, they must use resources efficiently. Individuals with a common self-interest form mutual–benefit organizations to fulfill the needs of their members. Commonweal organizations provide public services and are nonprofit. Public libraries and fire departments are examples of commonweal organizations.

Organizational Chart

An organizational chart is a diagram showing the structure of an organization with departments and leaders. The vertical hierarchy displays the lines of authority, or reporting relationships. The horizontal hierarchy may show departments of equivalent status but of differing functions. It represents the organization's division of labor. Employee interaction across a horizontal hierarchy for work-related reasons is called networking. Formal organizational charts are documented and show job titles. The lead positions displayed have nominal power. Informal charts are not documented and have natural leaders, due to particular personality traits, who possess real power.

Copyright © Mometrix Media. You have been licensed one copy of this document for personal use only. Any other reproduction or redistribution is strictly prohibited. All rights reserved.

Theories of Organization

A traditional view of organizational structure is a bureaucracy based on the assumption that a framework of rules will create a predictable environment. Also, efficiency is accomplished with a division of labor being directed by a proper hierarchy of authority. And finally, impersonality, the hiring and promoting of people based solely on their qualifications, increases competency. Authority in a traditional organization trickles from the top down, with its attention focused on tasks not people. This traditional closed-system ignores outside influences and creates fixed boundaries.

A modern view is that of an open-system, realizing outside influences, as from legal or economic environments, may affect the organization. Therefore, the organization has soft boundaries, allowing for interactions with other environments. More importantly it stresses the necessity for an organization to be flexible and adaptable to its unpredictable environment. The belief of equifinality, that there are several means by which a single goal may be achieved, is the fundamental principle to this view.

Departments

A functional department, such as a marketing or sales department, groups employees by the type of work they perform. This method of grouping allows for better communications and promotes opportunities, establishing more efficient methods of completing their tasks. A product or service department represents a mini entity that designs, manufactures, and markets a single product or provides a single service. Companies that offer multiple products or services may departmentalize this way. A department may be formed by geographical location. This allows managers to get a better understanding of the local market and consumer demands. A consumer type department may be created to better meet the needs of particular consumers. For example, a manufacturer may have one department that works solely with wholesalers while other department works with retailers. This would better accommodate the packaging, pricing, quantities, and shipping needs of its consumers. The notable disadvantage to product/service, location, and consumer type departments is that a duplication of certain tasks exists, which is inefficient and costly.

Management Theory

The universal process is the theory that one management process works for all organizations. The scientific management approach is focused on achieving efficiency by finding quantitative and objective methods for standardizing production operations. The operations management process creates and implements production procedures. Its focus is on changing raw materials into finished products. The general systems theory views organizations as a system of interrelated components that combine to form a whole greater in value than the sum of all the components. Contemporary management believes managers should be provided with training on staff planning, hiring, training, and reviewing to maintain consistency with the organization's structure and strategies.

Behavioral Methods

Behavioral scientist, Douglas McGregor, compared managers' traditional assumptions of people (Theory X) with his own views of people (Theory Y). Theory X assumes people are lazy and avoid work unless threatened or forced; that they prefer direction and are only interested in job security. In contrast, Theory Y assumes working comes natural to people, and they are energetic and willing to take responsibility; that they have self-direction and will do a good job if they are appropriately rewarded. Another behavioral scientist created Theory Z organizations, which combine American and Japanese management styles. They focus on the employee, encouraging long-term employment, assigning individual responsibilities, and including their opinions on decisions. Theory T and Theory T+ are similar theories that incorporate Southeast Asian philosophies about

Copyright © Mometrix Media. You have been licensed one copy of this document for personal use only. Any other reproduction or redistribution is strictly prohibited. All rights reserved.

work. Work has its importance but is not a goal in life. The goal in life is connected with God. People with authoritative positions represent God, and thus their goals should be achieved.

Contingency Management

Contingency management considers the tasks to be done and matches the appropriate individuals to complete them. Similarly, a contingency design theory on organizational structure considers its internal and external environments before matching an organizational strategy. One contingency model, the Burns and Stalker model, categorizes two types of organizations based on their environments.

Stable environments allow mechanistic organizations, which have rigid structures, formal communications, and limited, repetitive tasks with little knowledge requirements. Uncertain environments need organic organizations, which have adaptable and flexible structures, group communications, many tasks, requiring more knowledge, per individual.

Managerial Principles

Managers following the principle of equity base their decisions and actions on fairness and justice. The scalar chain is more commonly known as a chain of command, showing a succession of direct authority, such as a CEO has direct authority over executive managers who have direct authority over operational managers who have authority over employees, etc. Following this principle, subordinates are to report to their direct authority, not to an authority further up the chain. The unity of command principle feels it is important for each employee to have only one boss. The unity of direction is about making sure everyone is focusing in the same direction, or working towards the same goals.

Span of Control

The span of control refers to the number of people under a manager. It may either be narrow and tall or wide and flat. A work environment that has complex tasks or a broad diversity of tasks usually requires fewer employees per manager, thus a narrow span of control. As a result, more managers are needed, creating a tall hierarchy. In contrast, a work environment with simple tasks requiring little or no supervision may have a several employees under one manager, or a wide span of control. This structure requires fewer managers and creates a flat hierarchy.

Contingency Designs

Whether to have a centralized or decentralized organization is based on who is able to make the most informed decisions, upper-level management or lower-level management. Smaller organizations that have very few product changes and typically make uniform decisions would be suitable for a centralized structure. Larger organizations that thrive on product innovation and have to make many unique decisions would probably have more success as a decentralized organization. This would allow lower-level managers to make decisions on issues in which they have more knowledge and an invested interest.

Line and staff organizations follow the unity of command principle with line managers and staff each having its own chain of command. A line manager has authority over all the subordinates in his chain while a staff leader only has authority over his staff. The staff function is supportive of the line function.

A matrix organization has both vertical and horizontal lines of authority. This structure works in project environments where an employee reports to a functional manager (vertical authority) and a project manager (horizontal authority).

Copyright © Mometrix Media. You have been licensed one copy of this document for personal use only. Any other reproduction or redistribution is strictly prohibited. All rights reserved.

Organizational Changes

Organizational psychologists, David Nadler and Michael Tushman, describe four types of organizational changes based on their timing, whether they were anticipatory changes done prior to an expected occurrence or if they were reactionary changes following an unexpected event, and their magnitude, whether they were small incremental changes or huge strategic changes. They identified these changes as: tuning, adaptation, reorientation, and re-creation.

Tuning is the most common type of change. It is about implementing small changes to prevent anticipated problems.

Adaptation is the use of small changes in reaction to unexpected events.

Reorientation, also known as "frame bending", reshapes its company's strategy in anticipation of upcoming situations. It still pursues its company's original goal but in a vastly different way.

Re-creation, also known as "frame breaking", totally changes the company's mission and strategy as a result of unforeseen occurrences.

Resistance to Change

Educating employees on the necessity for the change may prevent resistance in the first place. By involving employees in the planning and/or execution of the changes, they are less likely to resist since they feel more connected to the process. If the resistance stems from fears and stress, management can alleviate these issues through providing training sessions, paid time off, or counseling for job-related anxiety. If only a small number of employees are resisting, management may be able to negotiate a deal, privately promising them something of value in exchange for their cooperation. Sometimes managers may manipulate successful changes by choosing the right time and amount of information to send out to key people. In desperate situations, when there is a shortage of time or funds, managers may have to coerce their employees by threatening their job security, annual increases, or promotions.

Organizational Development

Organizational development (OD) is a customized process to guide management on implementing changes. Its goals include: fostering employee awareness and alignment with the organization's goals, increasing communications and cooperation, developing a problem-solving environment, and encouraging participation. According to social psychologist, Kurt Lewin, there are three main phases in OD: unfreezing, change, and refreezing.

The unfreezing phase is about preparing employees for the change. By promoting the reasons for it, how it will be implemented, and its expected results. Various methods, such as announcements, meetings, and bulletins, may be used to accomplish this. To assess, or diagnose, employees' attitudes about the change, managers may check for changes in absenteeism, speak individually with employees, provide a questionnaire, and observe their behavior. The change phase is about correcting issues that may impede the process of change. There are various interventions that may be used to achieve this. The refreezing phase is about resolving unexpected problems, assessing the effectiveness of the change process, and doing follow-up checks.

Change Phase

The change phase is about correcting issues that may impede the process of change. This is achieved through intervention at individual, group, and organizational levels. One individual intervention includes having employees incorporate their personal goals in their career plans and showing them how the organization's success will help them achieve their own personal success.

Copyright © Mometrix Media. You have been licensed one copy of this document for personal use only. Any other reproduction or redistribution is strictly prohibited. All rights reserved.

Another individual intervention is aimed at developing employees' problem-solving and leadership skills, which nurtures a better understanding of the need for change.

Group interventions include clarifying job roles and duties on interdependent tasks, and to provide team building environments. According to statistical data, team building is the most effective OD intervention. One example of an organizational intervention is to reveal the results of a company-wide survey so that employees may compare their personal feelings with others'.

Preventing Conflicts

For controlling and preventing conflicts, organizations should provide managers with conflict management training, create appropriate policies and procedures to avoid ambiguities that could lead to conflict, and establish mechanisms for resolving grievances between management and its employees. Also, a manager's personalities and methods should be considered during hiring. Managers who are skilled communicators and openly listen to complaints rather than aggressively defend positions reduce unnecessary conflicts. And finally, creating working environments where a single goal may only be achieved through combined efforts promotes a harmonious environment. In contrast, win/lose competitions are best avoided since research indicates they often cause pointless conflicts.

Business Risk

Business risk refers to the uncertainties that could negatively impact a company's ability to stay operational; whereas an audit risk is the risk that an auditor may fail to detect a material weakness and consequently provide an inaccurate opinion. Audit risk may be reduced by doing more testing in an audit; however, this would also increase the audit costs. At some point the costs would outweigh the benefits, and so to some degree audit risk will always exist. Typically, having a 5% audit risk factor, and thus a 95% assurance factor, is considered acceptable.

Conflict Management

There are two types of conflict: realistic and unrealistic. Realistic conflicts occur from differing values, goals, or interests. They are resolved by first settling heightened emotions and then having the feuding parties work together on creating a solution. Unrealistic conflicts come from ignorance, misunderstanding, and stress. They are irrational arguments, which are destructive in nature and are best to be prevented. Conflict management is about accepting realistic conflicts, which social scientists believe bring personal growth and social evolution, while at the same time minimizing unrealistic conflicts.

Preventing Conflicts

There are several techniques for controlling and preventing conflicts on a personal level. For example, conflicts are less likely to take place when employees are aware of and avoiding behaviors that ignite conflicts, such as being over-bearing, critical, threatening, or partaking in name-calling. Other examples include listening better, increasing one's tolerance to others, reducing tension through exercise, considering all of the consequences before engaging in a conflict, and being more assertive to resolve misunderstandings right away rather than allowing them to build. Also taking one issue at a time, starting with the easiest ones and looking for win-win solutions, is less overwhelming and more productive.

Copyright © Mometrix Media. You have been licensed one copy of this document for personal use only. Any other reproduction or redistribution is strictly prohibited. All rights reserved.

Management Control System

A management control system refers to the methods and procedures established by management to efficiently and effectively achieve its goals. In addition to goals, the control system should have standards and an evaluation-reward system. Traditional management controls include using automated and manual methods of measuring, recording, and monitoring business operations.

Controls can be placed into three categories. Those that prevent unwanted outcomes are precontrol, also known as feed-forward controls. Some examples included training and budgeting. Controls used on an on-going basis, such as monitoring, are concurrent controls. And finally, controls used to compare actual performance with expected performance are postcontrol, or feed-back controls.

Contemporary Management Controls

Contemporary management controls have adopted other methods for measuring progress. The economic-value-added (EVA) financial control is obtained by subtracting the cost of capital invested in tangible assets from the firm's net operating profit. The market-value-added (MVA) control is determined by the market value minus all the invested capital. This difference shows the added value, or wealth, accumulated over market value. The activity-based costing (ABC) assigns a cost value to every activity necessary for producing a product or service. This allows managers to see the allocation of costs per product or service and allows them to determine which ones are more successful.

Open-Book Management

Open-book management reveals the firm's financial condition to employees and allows them to see how their jobs contribute to the firm. It provides a reward system based on the firm's success. The goal is to educate employees so they think like business owners in terms of the money flow. This helps them understand the need for efficiency.

The balanced scorecard system still uses traditional controls which have a financial emphasis, but also implores other controls that are focused on non-financial factors. For example, it monitors customer service to determine consumer retention and satisfaction. Thus, it has a balance of controls.

Multiple Controls

It is typical for multiple controls to be used towards achieving a particular objective. Here are the different possibilities for multiple control integration:

Combination controls refer to combining two or more controls, that used alone would be insufficient, but collectively are able to fulfill their duty. An example would be the combination of managerial reviews and the company's policies to ensure employees are completing their tasks in an appropriate manner.

Complementary controls are combining controls that would be effective on their own but realize a greater effectiveness when integrated. For example, security systems in a database may complement those found in the user software. Also manual controls and automated controls are commonly used as complementary companions.

Compensating controls uses strong controls in one area to account for the weak controls in another area. For example, if a third party has weak controls, then it is important to ensure there are strong in-house controls.

Copyright © Mometrix Media. You have been licensed one copy of this document for personal use only. Any other reproduction or redistribution is strictly prohibited. All rights reserved.

Assessing Controls

In order for an auditor to assess the controls of an operation, he needs a basis to compare them against. Typical benchmarks are generally accepted standards or principles, management's control philosophies and risk tolerance, and legal requirements.

An auditor may find situations where there is a duplication of controls or just too many, in which case he should recommend removing particular controls. If an auditor suspects a weakness, he must consider the entire audit environment because that weakness may be offset by a compensating control, or perhaps it may be only one part of a combination of controls that are collectively effective. If it still appears to be a weakness, there are a few things he must consider prior to making a recommendation. He must consider whether the operation is manual or automated, unique or standardized, and the amount of risk exposure. He may also consider doing a cost-benefit analysis for the implementation of a control.

Classification of Controls

Controls classified by their function include: directive, preventive, detective, corrective, manual, and computer controls.

Directive controls provide instruction, such as company policies.

Preventive controls are put in place to avoid undesirable occurrences. An authorization process could prevent employee fraud.

Detective controls are used to identify undesirable occurrence. They are the back-up system to preventive controls. A bank reconciliation is a detective control.

Corrective controls are used to fix an undesirable occurrence. Correction procedures and exception reports are corrective controls.

Manual controls refer to all non-automated controls, such as physical controls, budgets, company policies, and reports.

Computer controls are installed to authorize access and to ensure accuracy and completeness. They may be further classified as general controls and application controls. Examples of general computer controls are system software controls and data center operations controls. Application controls ensure transactions process completely and correctly and verify authorization. For example, computerized edit checks monitor data entry.

Controls classified by their objectives include: data completeness, data timeliness, data accuracy, and data authorization controls.

Data completeness controls ensure that the necessary data is present. Maintaining a transaction log is a data completeness control.

Controls that ensure the timeliness of data are important, as they help preserve its reliability and usefulness. An example would be the use of e-mail.

Controls for data accuracy verify that data is entered correctly and ensure it is not corrupted while it is being processed. Reconciliation reports are meant for data accuracy.

Data authorization controls require particular activities or transactions obtain managerial approval before they may be performed or processed.

Copyright © Mometrix Media. You have been licensed one copy of this document for personal use only. Any other reproduction or redistribution is strictly prohibited. All rights reserved.

Business Applications Systems

Data collection and input controls, as well as, processing controls are used to prevent corruptive alterations, errors, and omissions. They validate the data, ensuring its completeness and accuracy.

The various computer files where this information exists (i.e., transaction files, user files, command files, master file) must have controls to ensure they do not get erased, lost, or destroyed. Auditors must determine who has access to the files and who is responsible for updating them, as they hold valuable data, which is particularly useful for audit analysis.

The system's outputs, usually hard-copy documents and reports, require data output controls to ensure they are sent to the appropriate people in a timely fashion.

Data integrity controls are used to maintain that data is complete, accurate, consistent, timely, and properly authorized thereby ensuring it is reliable and usable.

Spreadsheet software is used to create spreadsheets on which decisions are based. Therefore, it is vital to maintain spreadsheet controls that ensure the software is adequately designed and documented and also to prevent improper usage or mistakes.

There must be documentation of the application system. It is a necessary learning tool for trainees and a reference guide for users and evaluators, auditors in particular. Documentation controls ensure the proper manuals are available and current. Typically, there are six types of manuals: systems, user, program, computer operations, help-desk, and network control.

During an audit, it is important to assess the application system's usability by surveying the user's satisfaction.

Preventive Controls

These business application system controls are preventive and focus on maintaining accuracy:

- Pre-coded forms/screens – These are forms or computer screens with fixed data fields, requiring the input of particular information. A similar control is referred to as pre-formatting.
- Brevity codes – These short codes are used to represent longer messages. For example, a frame shop may enter a customer order as "2BL", representing "two, black, large frames."
- System-assigned numbers – This is the sequential numbering of computerized documents.
- Turnaround documents – Such documents serve two purposes. First, they are used as notices to customers, such as a bill. After they are returned, they are used as input documents for data entry into the computer system.
- Two-person controls – One person observes or checks the other person's work to verify accuracy. These are typically used in high-risk activities.
- Validity checks – These controls check the accuracy of codes, such as those entered for states, customer numbers, or social security numbers. These controls are both preventive and detective.
- Compatibility tests – These are used to allow only authorized users into restricted areas. Using passwords is an example of this control.
- Concurrent access controls – These are used to prevent multiple users from accessing the same database file and trying to add or change data to it at the same time, which would potentially damage the file. An example of this control would be a program that denies access to all other users once a file has been opened.

- 71 -

Copyright © Mometrix Media. You have been licensed one copy of this document for personal use only. Any other reproduction or redistribution is strictly prohibited. All rights reserved.

- Management approvals – This requires important transactions entered on the system to obtain managerial approval by use of a passcode before being processed.
- Overrides – These controls prevent unauthorized employees from overriding errors. This is also a security control.

These business application system controls are preventive and focus on ensuring completeness:

- Data attribute checks – These controls verify that the data fields are completed correctly with respect to length and content.
- Pre-numbered forms – The sequential numbering of source and input documents alerts employees that documentation may be misplaced or lost.
- Transaction cancellation – This control rejects a transaction that has a document number which has already been used.

Detective Controls
These business application system controls are detective and focus on maintaining accuracy:

- Hash totals – In this control, a particular data field, such as the account numbers from all the documents in a batch, are totaled. The value is meaningless, but the number is used as a comparison with other hash totals.
- Limit check - This is a computer program that checks particular numeric fields, usually for quantity or dollar amounts, and limits their value to either one that does not go below a set number or above a set number. If the number is acceptable, it will be processed. If it is not, then the program will give an error message.
- Range test - This is similar to the limit check except it ensures particular numeric fields have both, high and low, limits. Similar controls include the range check and the discrete value check.
- Reasonableness test – This control uses computer programs to test the reasonableness of input data, calculated data, or output data by comparing it to another source document's data, historical data, or some other recorded standard.
- Check digit – This control uses a mathematical formula on a word or number (i.e., credit card or account numbers) to create a digit which is used to test and detect errors within transcription, transposition, and data entry and processing.
- Format checks – These verify that data is entered in the correct format, such as alphabetical or numeric digits.
- Sign test – This verifies a numeric data field has the correct positive or negative sign, as used with credits and debits.
- Field combination tests – These ensure that two or more particular data fields have correct correlating data, such as city and state or employee number and location.
- Header and trailer record verification – This ensures accuracy by comparing values in the first and last records of a file.
- Balance controls – These verify that a transaction's values are the same throughout all systems and functions.
- Descriptive read-back – When a code is entered, a message is retrieved and displayed on the screen for employee verification. For example, a business may enter an account number and have a customer's name and business history appear on the screen.
- Key verification – This ensures accuracy by requiring the user to re-key information, such as re-entering a user ID.
- One-for-one checking – To ensure accuracy and completeness, important output documents should be directly compared with the input documents.

- 72 -

Copyright © Mometrix Media. You have been licensed one copy of this document for personal use only. Any other reproduction or redistribution is strictly prohibited. All rights reserved.

- Batch totals – These are the computer system's automated control totals for quantities, line numbers, or dollars. To ensure correct data entry and processing, they are compared with the manually figured totals.
- Completeness test – This programmed control checks data fields for missing entries and to ensure no entries are made in those that are supposed to be left blank.
- Size test – This verifies the correct number of digits exists in a particular data field. This is commonly used for data fields requiring phone numbers, social security numbers, or zip codes.
- Sequence check – During data processing, this control keeps track of the transaction numbers. It will send an error message, notifying the user if there is a missing transaction.
- Duplicate checks – This program checks for duplicate records and notifies the user when they are detected.
- System matching – After matching transactions, such as customer order numbers to shipping numbers, the system reports any unmatched transactions for follow-up.
- Suspense file – Transactions that are no longer being processed due to detected errors are saved in a suspense file, awaiting corrections.
- Date checks – As transaction dates are recorded, these controls check for logical correlations. For example, a customer order date should be before a shipping date.
- Record counts – This control determines and compares available record counts with needed record counts to ensure a file will fit and information will not be lost.
- Run-to-run checking – In a series of program runs, each run totals the transactions and verifies that it is the same total as the previous run's total.
- Cross-field editing – Multiple data fields in the same record are checked for logical relationships. For example, it would verify that an area code is consistent with the zip code.
- Cross-record editing – This is similar to cross-field editing except the data fields being compared are in different records. For example, data fields in a transaction record may be checked for consistency with the fields in a master file.
- Comparison controls – These check for consistency among particular values in a record or multiple records. For example, it might check customer order dollar totals with amounts due on customer billings, reporting any discrepancies.

This is a detective control ensuring security:

- System logging – For auditing purposes, the system keeps a log of transactions with recorded dates, times, user and terminal IDs, and department numbers.

Corrective Controls

These business application systems controls are corrective and focus on maintaining accuracy:

- Error report – this lists all unprocessed transactions due to errors and provides instruction for fixing the errors.
- Exception report – Departures from typical values, quantities, or procedures prompts the system to produce an exception report.
- Control report – This includes batch totals for manual reconciliation and system logging reports for verification.
- Error totals – This control identifies the type of error and the location of where it originates, making employees aware of reoccurring mistakes so that they may improve their productivity.

Copyright © Mometrix Media. You have been licensed one copy of this document for personal use only. Any other reproduction or redistribution is strictly prohibited. All rights reserved.

These business application system controls are corrective and focus on maintaining continuity:

- Automatic error correction – The computer system is preprogrammed with set criteria allowing it to automatically correct errors.
- Clear and complete error messages – Having easy to understand error messages allows for faster corrections.
- Documentation – System analysts, programmers, and users may refer to appropriate manuals for solving problems with the computer system.
- Transaction back-out – In the event of a processing error, this control allows a user to back out of the transaction. Most application systems have this control.

Problem Solving

A problem is the difference between an actual situation and the desired situation. An auditor's findings reveal the actual state of things while their recommendations suggest changes for obtaining the desired state.

Problem-solving process:

1. Identify the real problem, not just symptoms. The severity of the problem should be determined, as well. A small controversy is considered to be a stable issue, which may be easily fixed. A dynamic issue is one with a lot of controversy, requiring a group's input to solve. A problem with an extreme amount of conflict is a critical issue and needs to be resolved by senior management.
2. Create a suitable list of possible solutions.
3. Evaluate the possible solutions to determine which one would solve the problem's root cause most efficiently and effectively.
4. Develop a detailed plan for implementing the chosen solution. The necessary resources must be acquired and employees notified of their required actions. Once implementation is complete, the affected product and process should be evaluated to see if the desired goal was reached.

Resolving, Solving and Dissolving

Problems may be dealt with in one of the following manners: resolved, solved, or dissolved. To resolve a problem means to gather just enough information to make a quick fix that is suffice but not optimal. Making a fast decision like this requires relying on one's opinions, and therefore uses a qualitative, subjective approach. Solving a problem, on the other hand, means taking the time to research many possible solutions and selecting the best one, characterized as having an optimal balance of resources and benefits. The necessary research is quantitative in nature. To dissolve a problem, the circumstances which created the problem in the first place are changed so that the problem no longer exists. This requires both qualitative and quantitative methods.

Prospective Methods

Auditors use retrospective methods to analyze past performances to assess the current status. These methods use administrative records, surveys, interviews, and observations to gather research to help solve problems with existing issues and policies.

Also, auditors are often asked to anticipate future conditions, such as future costs, issues, or needed resources; as well as, to find ways to improve the future, as by determining the potential success of

Copyright © Mometrix Media. You have been licensed one copy of this document for personal use only. Any other reproduction or redistribution is strictly prohibited. All rights reserved.

particular asset acquisitions and divestitures. Dealing with future issues requires using prospective methods. These methods can fit into four categories:

- Actual Prospective Methods – This involves doing pilot tests, or experimental tests of potential approaches.
- Empirical Prospective Methods – These include analyzing simulations and making forecasts.
- Logical Prospective Methods – Risk assessments, system analyses, and the creation of "what-if" scenarios fall into this category.
- Judgmental Prospective Methods – This type includes obtaining opinions from experts or using the Delphi technique to receive independent views among group members.

Brainstorming Technique

The purpose of brainstorming is to compile a huge number of ideas. To encourage participation, the group members' inhibitions are dissolved by suspending the evaluation of ideas until a later phase and prohibiting criticism. Also, all ideas, no matter how outlandish, are to be recorded; as unrealistic ideas may spark useful ideas from others. Participants are encouraged to expand on others' ideas, also known as hitchhiking. In addition to generating ideas, the interaction within a brainstorming group also encourages teamwork and allows a consensus to be more readily reached.

It should be noted, however, that researchers have found nominal groups to be even more successful at generating ideas. The nominal group technique (NGT) gathers ideas from a group of 5-8 participants who are not allowed to communicate to each other, as they are given time to silently formulate ideas. This method works well with a highly diversified group. Diversity may include varied educations, backgrounds, or working at different levels throughout the organization.

Synectics

Synectics is the method of using nontraditional activities to form an environment that induces creativity and ultimately fresh approaches to solving a problem. This typically works best for a small group (6-8 members). Examples of nontraditional activities include:

- Excursions and fantasies – The purpose is to give participants a break from consciously focusing on a problem. The change in environment energizes them while their subconscious continues to work on the problem.
- Problem-solving Analogies – Participants are given a checklist of types of analogies to consider. These include:
- Personal Analogy – Participants compare current problems to similar problems of the past & use their previous experiences to solve current issues.
- Direct Analogy – Members consider various settings where the problematic function would not be problematic.
- Symbolic Analogy – The comparisons involve symbols, figures, or pictures.
- Attribute Analogy – Participants are given a list of attributes belonging to an object, such as color, function, or an icon. For each attribute, they write down the free association that comes to them.

Copyright © Mometrix Media. You have been licensed one copy of this document for personal use only. Any other reproduction or redistribution is strictly prohibited. All rights reserved.

Problem-Solving Systems Analysis

A problem-solving systems analysis deals with a problem by dissecting it into smaller problems. The following three assumptions are considered during the search for possible solutions:

- Systems are open – This means they are interactive with the environment. The hierarchical, input-output, and entities models represent open systems. The hierarchical model views systems as part of an order of systems. The input-output model focuses on the process of how inputs transform into finished outputs. The entities model studies the interactions of group members.
- Problems often have multiple causes – The identification of multiple causes allows the problem to be solved from different positions, increasing the probability of success.
- Big picture perspective is important – To widen the possibilities of solutions, it is important to consider how the system functions in the grand scheme of operations; as too narrow of a focus may be limiting.

Force-Field Analysis

Force-field analysis first defines the problem, and then categorizes relative forces as: inhibiting or facilitating. Inhibiting forces hinder a problem from being solved while facilitating forces bring it closer to being solved. Once these forces are identified, strategies must be developed to minimize the inhibiting ones and increase facilitating ones. This type of analysis may be done with any group size but should have a leader to help the team rank the forces and solutions.

A T- analysis is similar in nature. A large "T" is drawn and used to visually segregate strengths and weaknesses, as each is written on opposite sides of the "T". Focus is then placed on diminishing the weaknesses

Various Techniques

Problem-solving techniques:

- Attribute Listing – An item's or situation's qualities are listed, and each one is carefully scrutinized to determine if alterations to it may prove beneficial.
- Morphological Analysis – New approaches toward a solution are sought by studying how various elements of a problem interrelate.
- Imagineering – This means to visualize how a complicated process may be done perfectly with no wastage. Action is taken, and the results are compared to the imagined ideal process so that the action may be modified in an attempt to replicate the ideal process.
- Leapfrogging – To take mammoth strides toward creating idealistic solutions for a problem.
- Value-Analysis – The study of a process or product to determine how it may be performed or manufactured at a lower cost without compromising quality. This type of analysis may be done as a group using brainstorming, hitchhiking, or leapfrogging techniques.
- Delphi Technique – In lieu of meeting face-to-face, each group member anonymously writes suggestions. All suggestions are collected. The compiled results are then dispersed to each group member to make further comments. The process repeats until a consensus is reached.
- Blasting, Creating, and Refining – To view something in a totally new way and create fresh, original ideas.
- Edisonian – A solution is sought by means of trial-and-error. The technique is named after the famous inventor, Thomas Edison, who achieved success using it.
- Investigative Questioning – To acquire a better understanding of a problem and its primary cause, six investigating questions should be asked: who, what, why, where, when, and how.

- 76 -

Copyright © Mometrix Media. You have been licensed one copy of this document for personal use only. Any other reproduction or redistribution is strictly prohibited. All rights reserved.

- Cause and Effect (C&E) Diagrams – These are useful for identifying a problem's possible causes. They are used by continually asking the question, "Why?" to a problem. After five or six times of asking that question, the root cause becomes evident. Auditors use C&E diagrams to explain their audit findings and to include the auditee in the process by having them confirm the causes identified.
- Pareto Charts – These charts group data and visually show the relative importance of each group. They are used to understand how the 80/20 rule, which states 80% of the problems are attributed to 20% of the sources, applies.
- Psychodramatic Approaches – Role-playing and role-reversal are used to understand problems. When an individual's problem is being studied in this way, it is called psychodrama; when a group's problems are being studied, it is referred to as sociodrama.
- Operations Research – This is a discipline, by which mathematical operations are used to determine the best solutions for business problems.

Decision Making

Environment of Certainty

Decision-making methods in an environment of certainty:

- Dominance Method – Of all possible choices in a decision, the one that is the most dominating is selected. For one choice to dominate another, its individual components must be as good as the other choice's components *and* have at least one better component.
- Additive Weighing Method – Each decision's components have an ordered valued and are assigned a weighted value; components of more importance receive heavier weights. The numeric value of each component is multiplied by its weighted value. The sum of all the components' individual scoring is totaled for each decision's overall score. The decision with the highest overall score is selected.
- Effectiveness Index Method – This method thoroughly analyzes the situation. While the other methods isolate the individual components of a decision to value them, the Effectiveness Index method also takes their interactions into account. This method is best when there are strong interactions between the components of the decisions or if making the wrong decision would be too costly.
- Lexicographic Method – The components of a decision's choices are put into an order of importance. The most important components are then compared among the different choices. If two of the choices have components of equal value, then the second most important components are compared. This continues until the components of one choice are deemed more important than the others'. This method is best to use when one component of a decision is of greater concern than the other components.
- Satisficing Method – A minimum standard must be determined for each of the decisions' components. If a decision does not meet the minimum standards, it is rejected. The first decision that is able to meet all the standards is chosen. This method is not designed to find the best choice, but rather the first one that will work. This is an inexpensive method to use when there are many choices and having the best choice is unimportant.

Types of Decisions

- Sequential decisions – Decisions that may only be made after prior related decisions are made. For example, deciding what type of manufacturing equipment to purchase is dependent on the decision of which product components will be produced and which will be purchased. Typically decided by lower-level managers

Copyright © Mometrix Media. You have been licensed one copy of this document for personal use only. Any other reproduction or redistribution is strictly prohibited. All rights reserved.

- Non-sequential decisions – Decisions that may be made independently from other decisions. Upper-level managers typically make these decisions.
- Structured, programmed decisions – These decisions follow a routine response, requiring very little human involvement. Knowing when to reorder raw materials would be an example. Such decisions are common for lower-level managers who deal with an organization's operations.
- Unstructured, non-programmed decisions – These are unique decisions, not following any rules for making them. They are typical for an upper-level manager who focuses on an organization's competitive strategies.

Decision Environments

- Decisions with certainty – All the facts about the situation are known, and every possible decision choice has only one definite outcome.
- Decisions with risk – The choices in a decision have more than one possible outcome, but the probabilities of each one happening are known.
- Decisions with uncertainty – The choices in a decision have more than one possible outcome, but the chances of each happening are unknown.
- Decisions with conflict – Decisions which involve the actions of competitors.
- Deterministic data- Data that is historically known to be true, in which there is one outcome for the possible actions. This type of data is used when the decision being made is in a predictable and stable environment.
- Probabilistic data – Data that estimates the possible outcomes of a decision and assigns a probability of each one occurring. It is used to help evaluate decision alternatives when risk and uncertainty are present in unpredictable and unstable environments.

Decision with Risk

A decision with risk means there are many possible outcomes and the probabilities of each happening are known. The best approach for making a decision under these circumstances is to select the action which has the highest expected value, using this formula:

$$\text{Expected Value Action A}$$
$$= \text{Probability of outcome A} \times \text{Value of outcome A}$$
$$+ \text{Probability of outcome B} \times \text{Value of outcome B}$$

Uncertain Environment

Making a decision in uncertain circumstances means there is no way to calculate the probabilities of the different possible outcomes happening. Therefore, the decision maker must use his own judgment in determining the various probabilities of each outcome happening. Under the Mini-max strategy, he would then calculate the expected value of an action using values of a worst-case scenario (row minima). The action with the highest expected value, based on worst-case numbers would be selected. The decision maker would expect this value as a minimum, knowing there is a chance for a greater value. Using the Maxi-max strategy, he would calculate the expected value of an action using values based on a best-case scenario (row maxima). Again, the action with the highest expected value would be chosen. This time, the value would represent the best possible value the decision maker could obtain, with a chance of it being lower.

Copyright © Mometrix Media. You have been licensed one copy of this document for personal use only. Any other reproduction or redistribution is strictly prohibited. All rights reserved.

Game Theory

Game theory is the process for making a decision in a conflicting, or competitive, environment. It considers an opponent's strategies when determining an action's possible outcomes while using the Mini-max strategy of decision-making. There are two types of games in competition:

- Zero-sum games – In this situation, one opponent gains at the other opponent's expense. The sum of each players' gains and losses will equal zero (i.e., competitor A has 4 victories, and competitor B has 4 losses (+4 – 4 = 0)).
- Nonzero-sum games – In this situation, an opponent's gains are not at the total expense of another opponent. This type of game is more common in business, such as with contract bidding, product development, and product pricing.

Decision-Making Tools

The main difference between decision-making and problem-solving is that decision-making focuses on a choice that effects the future; whereas, problem-solving is about changing a situation that began in the past.

Decision-making tools:

- Differential Analysis: A comparison of revenues/costs among different options.
- Discriminant Analysis: A subjective method for distinguishing effective actions from ineffective actions.
- Cost-benefit Analysis: Expected costs are subtracted from the expected benefits for each alternative. The choice with the greatest value is chosen.
- Flowchart: A diagram depicting the order of events, choices, and possible outcomes in a complex situation.
- Decision Trees: A diagram displaying the sequential order of events, choices, and possible outcomes. Unlike a flowchart, it also includes the probabilities of the various outcomes happening.
- Payoff Table: A table showing the values of the gains or losses for the various outcomes of a decision's choices.
- Activity Analysis: Using a T-column, activities-of-value are segregated from activities-of-no value. The objective is to minimize, if not completely eliminate, the activities-of-no value.
- Risk Analysis: A T-column is used to list possible risks on one side and ways to overcome those risks on the other side.
- Success-Failure Analysis: Situations that are sure to bring success are written on one side of a T-column while those that are sure to cause failure are on the other side.
- Reality Check: a T-column is used to separate expected risks from potential concerns.

Copyright © Mometrix Media. You have been licensed one copy of this document for personal use only. Any other reproduction or redistribution is strictly prohibited. All rights reserved.

Plan Engagements

Working Papers

The main purpose for working papers is to document the fieldwork that is necessary for making conclusions and recommendations. They are also used to monitor the audit's progression and supervise the team's work. Additionally, they allow others, such as the auditee, external auditors, and government auditors, to examine the audit's quality.

With legal advisement, organizational policies should be developed to determine the retention and destruction of working papers. Typically, working papers are discarded after they are of no use. They are not to be kept indefinitely, not even those which involve fraud.

The contents of the working papers should include the audit's objectives, scope, methodology, evaluation criteria, documentation of the fieldwork, and proof of supervisory reviews. Standard notations include headings, work completion dates, auditor initials, and index numbers for cross-referencing purposes. They are complete when they fulfill the audit objectives, and they are sufficient when an auditor, who is unaffiliated with the project, is able to understand the work completed which led to the conclusions and recommendations.

Working papers may be created on paper or electronically. If they are electronic, controls must be established for preserving and securing the data. For example, back-up copies should be saved, and controls allowing only the original auditor to make changes to the papers should be installed.

Audit Reports

Audit reports should include these essential items:

- Objectives – To define the parameters of the audit.
- Scope – To describe the sources of evidence and the extent of their examination, the location and timing of the audit work, as well as, any limitations, such as unreasonable time constraints or restricted access to data.
- Methodology – To explain the method used to collect, test, and analyze data.
- Findings and Conclusions - To share significant findings relevant to each objective. Insignificant findings, which would not be in the audit report, should still be communicated to management in writing.
- Recommendations – To convince the auditee to follow suggested directive action for the purpose of correcting or improving a current weakness.
- Compliance with Standards – To express that the auditors followed proper standards while conducting the audit.
- Compliance with Laws and Regulations – To report any indications of significant noncompliance with laws or regulations by an auditee.
- Management's Response – To reflect the auditee's feelings about the auditor's conclusions and recommendations. If they are in disagreement with the findings but seem valid, the auditor may adjust the audit report accordingly. If they seem invalid, the auditor may include a response to management's response.
- Noteworthy Accomplishments – To recognize management's significant achievements. This adds balance to the report and may encourage other managers to strive for improved results.

Copyright © Mometrix Media. You have been licensed one copy of this document for personal use only. Any other reproduction or redistribution is strictly prohibited. All rights reserved.

<u>Deficient Audit Finding</u>

The following items must be included when reporting a deficient audit finding: criteria, condition, cause, and effect. Criteria are standards used as a benchmark for evaluating. They may be professional standards, industry standards, historical performance, or management goals. The auditor must use due professional care in selecting the appropriate criteria and is expected to disclose which criteria he used. The condition, or the current situation during the time of the audit, should be stated. The cause of the deficiency is the reason the condition is not able to meet the expectations listed in the criteria. The auditor must provide sufficient evidence and a reasonable explanation, connecting the deficiency to the alleged cause. The effect is the condition's deviation from the criteria. An evaluation of the effect is not necessarily required in an audit report. However, if an effect is deemed significant, a recommendation should be provided.

<u>Well Written</u>

A well written audit report should be easy to read and understand, organized in a logical format, using simple terminology. Abbreviations and acronyms should be avoided, but if necessary, they must be defined. To convey complex information, visual diagrams, pictures, or charts may be used. Every bit of information should be accurate, particularly the findings and conclusions. A single inaccuracy may cause the user to doubt the entire report. Also, the report should be written objectively. Presenting facts in an unbiased fashion and providing balanced viewpoints (management's responses to findings, conclusions, and recommendations) adds credibility to the report. To prompt corrective action, it must present the findings in such a way that the reader is convinced that the related conclusions and recommendations are logical. And finally, it should be concise, so the reader does not get bored and miss the main points.

If the auditor agrees to keep management apprised of the audit's progress, if the audit scope is being modified, or if the auditor detects an inefficiency that is insignificant but feels it is something the operational manager should be aware of, a written interim report would appropriately convey this information.

Significant findings that require immediate attention may be orally reported to those that have the authority to take corrective action. A written account of the oral report and the reason for not creating a written one should be recorded.

Summary reports highlight the audit findings. These typically accompany the full written audit reports distributed to senior management and the audit committee.

<u>Errors</u>

If a significant error or omission is detected in an audit report after it has been distributed, the chief audit executive (CAE) must provide corrected information to each party who received a copy of the original audit report. If an audit is affected by an auditor's noncompliance with the International Standards for the Professional Practice of Internal Auditing, the audit results should disclose which specific standards were not complied with, the reason for not complying with them, and the impact this had on the audit.

Audit Techniques

Conventional audit techniques use computer-assisted audit techniques (CAAT), which may include the use of generalized audit software, the test data method, tracing, extended records, and utility programs to evaluate simple, batch application systems. Little technical knowledge of data processing is required. Auditors test controls periodically, mostly using test data. Concurrent audit techniques include: integrated test facility (ITF), system control review file (SCARF), simulation,

Copyright © Mometrix Media. You have been licensed one copy of this document for personal use only. Any other reproduction or redistribution is strictly prohibited. All rights reserved.

snapshots, and audit hooks. They are designed for evaluating online systems or more complex application systems. It is recommended for auditors to have a higher level of technical knowledge of data processing to facilitate these techniques. Concurrent auditing mostly uses real data for control testing on a continual basis.

Phases of an Audit

The five phases of an audit include: preliminary survey, audit program, fieldwork, reporting, and monitoring/follow-up. The preliminary phase is about the auditor acquainting himself with the audit environment. The next phase is about creating an audit program which documents the necessary audit procedures, such as reviewing certain files or testing particular controls, in order to meet the audit's objectives. The procedures are followed during the fieldwork phase. Upon conclusion of the fieldwork, the reporting phase begins. The auditor's opinion, along with all the gathered evidence which led to that opinion, is put into a report. The auditee receives a copy of the report, which is discussed during the exit conference. The final phase of monitoring/follow-up concludes the audit process. The audit director should follow-up after an audit to ensure corrective actions are being facilitated and are obtaining desired results.

Survey Phase

During the preliminary survey phase, the auditor must acquaint himself with the audit environment. He should inspect equipment, observe procedures, ask questions, review documents, identify potential risk exposures and controls, determine the appropriate standards to use for evaluation, and understand the environment's objectives. Questionnaires and employee interviews may be used to obtain general information of the area and to learn of any concerns about controls. An entrance conference should be held with the auditee to discuss the objectives and scope of the audit and to inform the auditee of what personnel and records will be needed during the process. Also estimated start and finish dates should be provided. At the end of this phase, an audit budget should be finalized. If by the end of the preliminary survey, the auditor concludes that the area is operating as it should and if audit resources are stretched, he may report the preliminary survey results with notification that the audit has been canceled.

Fieldwork Phase

The procedures established in the audit program are followed during the fieldwork phase. Operations, records, and controls are evaluated against a standard and documented in working papers along with other evidence gathered, all of which is used by the auditor to formulate an opinion. During the preliminary survey phase, concerns may have been relayed through questionnaires and interviews, as well as, discoveries of uncorrected deficiencies previously mentioned in prior audits. Those issues would be investigated during this phase of fieldwork. Also, as the fieldwork progresses, it may be decided that additional work or changes need to be incorporated into the audit procedures.

Auditor Recommendations

If corrective actions are not taking place, the audit director should notify higher management. Their influence will usually ensure corrective actions are implemented in a timely fashion. Audit recommendations should only be considered closed if the deficiency is fixed either by the recommendation or some other action being implemented, or if the deficiency no longer exists due to changing circumstances, or if management would rather assume the risk. In the latter situation, the severity of the risk should determine whether the recommendations should be pursued at a later time.

Copyright © Mometrix Media. You have been licensed one copy of this document for personal use only. Any other reproduction or redistribution is strictly prohibited. All rights reserved.

<u>Tasks</u>

The audit director puts together an audit team with the appropriate skills for a specific audit. He approves needed resources and attends the entrance conferences. The final audit report is given to him for his review, and he may determine if more fieldwork is needed. Afterwards, he attends the exit conference, and then monitors the auditee's progress on implementing corrective action. He assesses the team's job performance, and finally closes the audit. The managing supervisor begins by approving the proposed budget and attending the entrance conference. He reviews and approves the audit program, and then delegates duties to the auditors. Throughout the fieldwork process, he offers guidance and reviews their working papers. Once an audit report is drafted, he checks it over. He attends the exit conference and plans follow-up reviews. Prior to closing the audit, he assesses the auditors' performances.

The team leader determines how many budgeted hours each team member gets for completing their assigned tasks. He attends the entrance conference and drafts the audit program. After reviewing the working papers, he prepares the audit report and attends the exit conference. Lastly, he assesses his team's job performance. The staff runs the preliminary survey and attends the entrance conference. They help develop the drafted audit program created by their leader. Afterwards, they follow the program, completing all necessary fieldwork. Their final tasks are contributing to the audit report and attending the exit conference.

<u>Analytical Techniques</u>

While reviewing the company's financial and operational figures, the following analyses are used to determine the reasonableness of the data:

- Regression analysis - By determining one variable's relationship to other variables, logical conclusions may be drawn. For example, if product prices (variable A) were lowered, then it is reasonable to expect the number of sales (variable B) to have risen.
- Ratio analysis – This is the comparison of different financial statement numbers, such as dividing the current assets by current liabilities to determine if the firm has enough money to cover its short-term debts. A variety of ratios may be figured and subsequently used for comparison with ratios calculated from prior years, competitors, or industrial averages.
- Trend analysis – This compares a company's financial ratios over a period of time. By establishing a historical pattern, logical expected values may be determined.

Evidence

<u>Obtaining Documents</u>

To legally obtain documents, a subpoena or search warrant must be issued unless voluntary consent has been given. Courts and grand juries issue subpoenas. There are three types. A regular subpoena summons a witness. A subpoena duces tectum requests the presence of documents and records to be at a grand jury or deposition at a set time. And a forthwith subpoena is served by surprise so no opportunity is given for documents to be fabricated, changed, or destroyed. Only an agent of the court or grand jury may examine subpoenaed documents.

To request a search warrant, usually an affidavit is filled out, explaining the reasons for the request and providing a location in which the evidence is believed to exist. If a judge is convinced there is probable cause for believing the documents are connected to a crime, he will issue a search warrant. The simplest method of obtaining documents is through voluntary consent. Although the consent may be given orally, it is best to get it in writing.

Copyright © Mometrix Media. You have been licensed one copy of this document for personal use only. Any other reproduction or redistribution is strictly prohibited. All rights reserved.

Acceptance of a Document

Documenting fraud is a continuous process throughout the entire fraud investigation. When obtaining documents for evidence in an investigation, it is best to collect originals, if possible, and to make copies to work with while retaining the originals in a safe location. It is best to minimize the need to touch originals, as the investigation may require forensic analysis of them.

Organizing the documents for quick referencing is particularly necessary in cases with a large number of documents. They should be sorted by witness or transaction with a "high priority" file, containing the most relevant documents. A database may also be used for organization. The document's date, a brief description of it, from whom and when it was collected, and individuals involved with the activities related to the document should be included in the database. To have a document accepted in court it must be a relevant and material piece of evidence, properly identified, with proof of its chain of custody.

Documents in a Fraud Investigation

A great deal of fraud occurs from altering, destroying, duplicating, or fabricating fictitious documents. Therefore, examining the documents of transactions is a necessary procedure for gathering fraud evidence. Transactions usually begin with a source document, such as an invoice or check, and leave a paper trail through the accounting records, such as entries in the general ledger, postings into individual accounts, and cumulative amounts in the financial statements. Investigating a value thought to be understated in the financial statements should begin by examining source documents and following the paper trail forward to the statements. An investigation of a value thought to be overstated in the financial statements should begin by examining the financial statements and following the paper trail backwards to the source documents.

Types of Evidence

Evidence can be categorized as follows:

- Direct evidence is factual proof of something.
- Circumstantial evidence is proof of one thing which infers through logical deduction evidence of something else.

For example, suppose allegations are made about an employee stealing expensive office equipment. Direct evidence would be finding the equipment, identified by its serial number, at the employee's house while acting on a search warrant. Circumstantial evidence would be the employee's bank statement showing a deposit made two days after the equipment was stolen for an amount equal to the equipment's approximate value.

Documentation of an Interview

During a fraud investigation, documentation of an interview should include the date, identity of the interviewer, and whether it took place over the phone or in person. To maintain confidentiality, the interviewee should be referred to as a symbol number (i.e., I-22) in the report. This symbol number is for cross-referencing into a secured file where all the interviewee identities are kept.

To indicate the quality of information given, a brief background of the interviewee, stating his job position or expertise, should be added. If payment is given for information, the amount must be disclosed. Notations of facts, dates, quotes, and possible evidence should be made during the interview. At the end of the interview, these notes should be reconfirmed with the witness to

- 84 -

Copyright © Mometrix Media. You have been licensed one copy of this document for personal use only. Any other reproduction or redistribution is strictly prohibited. All rights reserved.

ensure accuracy. The interview should be transcribed into writing as soon as possible while the facts are fresh in the interviewer's mind.

<u>Fraud Report</u>

According to IIA Standards, a fraud report containing findings, conclusions, recommendations, and corrective actions must be issued in writing at the end of the investigative phase. Other sources recommend the fraud report include a cover page, documentation of witnesses, working papers, and an index. The cover page should have a case file number; case status (i.e., pending/closed); the date; a brief description of the case, including the reasons for it; identity of the lead investigator, as well as, the alleged guilty party; whether the case was criminal, civil, or administrative; the investigation's costs; and the estimated losses resulting from the corruption. The report should include documentation of only relevant witnesses. Summarized working papers may be in the report, or the papers may be included as attachments to it. An index, chronologically ordered, is useful. A cover letter addressing the party who requested the investigation should accompany the report. It should state the alleged violation that was investigated and summarize witness testimonials.

Gathering Information

Observations, unobtrusive measures, and anecdotal records are all means by which an auditor may gather information. An observation is made by directly watching a situation and the people involved. While auditors may find it advantageous to directly observe body language, they should be cautioned to recognize its limitation; people may alter their behavior when they know they are being watched. Using an unobtrusive measure removes this limitation, as the auditor inconspicuously observes the actions of employees without their knowledge. This method is particularly helpful for determining if employees are complying with policies and procedures. For example, the auditor may be standing in an unnoticeable spot secretly observing whether manufacturing employees are complying with safety goggle requirements. Anecdotal records are written descriptions of specific situations. Examples include a manager's account of the handling of a customer complaint or an employee evaluation supported by specific examples of the employee's behavior.

Sampling Methods

Random Sampling is the simplest of statistical sampling methods, by which every item in the population has the same probability of being picked to represent the population. This selection process may be done using a computer program or with random number tables. Use of a random number table requires starting at a random point on the table and selecting the numbers that read across or down until the desired sample size is reached. The population's items with the corresponding numbers form the sample. Other statistical sampling methods include systematic sampling and cluster sampling.

Using the systematic sampling method, the population is divided by the desired sample size, dropping any decimals that result. The quotient is the uniform sampling interval. For example, dividing a population of 600 by a desired sample of 100 would create a uniform sampling interval of 6. A number between 1 and the uniform sampling interval is selected from a random number table to obtain a random starting number. That number and every number per uniform interval that follows becomes part of the sample. (i.e., If 4 is randomly chosen between 1 and 6, the first sample item would be number 4, followed by every 6th number thereafter, such as 10, 16, 22, and so on.) This method should be used when the population's units are not numerically sequenced. Other statistical sampling methods include random sampling and cluster sampling.

Copyright © Mometrix Media. You have been licensed one copy of this document for personal use only. Any other reproduction or redistribution is strictly prohibited. All rights reserved.

The cluster sampling method is used when the sample units of a population contain a group, or cluster, of elements, such as data files, business units, or branch offices. There are three degrees of cluster sampling: one-stage, two-stage, and three stage sampling. One-stage sampling randomly selects the sample clusters. It is used for small-sized clusters that are simplistic. Two-stage sampling uses the randomly selected clusters to randomly select specific units within each cluster. This is used for large-sized clusters that are moderately complex. Three-stage sampling takes a random sample of clusters, and then takes a sample of units within the sample, and finally selects a sample of a particular element (object, thing, or unit) within those units. This three-stage sampling is used for large-sized clusters that are highly complex. Other statistical sampling methods include systematic sampling and cluster sampling.

Attribute Sampling vs. Variable Sampling

The purpose of attribute sampling is to calculate the frequency of a particular attribute, or characteristic, occurring in a population. Sample units having a certain attribute are counted, such as the number of reimbursed travel expenses exceeding allowable limits, and then presented as a percentage of the population. Attribute sampling is usually used for compliance testing, and it is a method mostly used by internal auditors.

The purpose of variable sampling is to measure a quantifiable value, such as by weight, length, or dollar amount. An example of a variable to be measured would be the average dollar amount paid to travel expense claims exceeding allowable limits. Variable sampling is used for substantive testing, and it is a method mostly used by external auditors. The required sample size for estimating variables is usually larger than that needed for estimating attributes.

Attribute Sampling

The formula for attribute sampling is:

Estimated percentage of uniques with attribute (p) =

Number of units with attribute (a) / Total number of sample units (n)

Estimated No. of units in population with attribute = Total Population (N) x Estimated Percentage with attribute (p)

Example: An auditor wants to determine the percentage of unauthorized long distance phone calls made in the last year. There is a total population of 5000 long distance calls, from which he picks 100 of them as a sample. He discovers 4 of the 100 long distance calls were unauthorized. Therefore, the estimated percentage of unauthorized long distance calls would be: $p = a / n = 4 / 100 = 0.04 = 4\%$

Applying this estimated rate of occurrence to the entire population of calls would mean an estimated 200 long distance calls were unauthorized, calculated as follows:

Est. total # of units with attribute = N x p = 5000 x 0.04 = 200 calls

Sampling Error

The formula for calculating the sampling error for an attribute sampling is:

$$E_p = t \sqrt{(pq/n)}$$

E_p = Sampling Error of the estimated percentage of units with a particular attribute

Copyright © Mometrix Media. You have been licensed one copy of this document for personal use only. Any other reproduction or redistribution is strictly prohibited. All rights reserved.

t = value from tables, corresponding to confidence level

(i.e., for 90% confidence level, t = 1.645; 95% confidence level, t = 1.96;

99% confidence level, t = 2.58)

p= Estimated percentage of units with the attribute

q= The compliment of p, in other words q = 1- p

n = number of sample units

To determine the sampling error as a number for the population, the formula is:

$$E_i \ = E_p \text{ x Total Population}$$

Attribute Sampling Size

To calculate an attribute sampling size, the formula is:

Sample Size (n) = ((t value)^2 x est. % with attribute (p) x Compliment of p(q)) /Error (E)^{2T} Tolererance

Example: From an original sample of 100 out of a population of 5000 long distance calls, an auditor discovers 4% were unauthorized. With a 90% confidence level, this meant 200 calls, plus or minus 160 calls (a 3.2% error tolerance), were unauthorized. To determine what sample size would be needed to get results with a lower error tolerance, say 2%, the auditor must use the formula.

$$n = (t^2pq) \text{ / } E^2 = (1.645)^2(0.04)(0.96) \text{ / } (0.02)^2 = 260$$

Therefore, to ensure a higher precision on the results (the error tolerance reduced to 2%), the auditor must add 160 sample units to his original 100 to have a total sample size of 260 units.

Sampling Error

The following formula is used to calculate the sampling error for variable sampling:

Sampling Error (E_y) = (t value x standard deviation(s)) / $\sqrt{\text{sample size (n)}}$

Example: The auditor would like to estimate the amount spent on supply requisitions in a year. From a population of 1000 requisition forms, he selects a sample of 100. For a 95% confidence level, the t-value is 1.96. He calculates the standard deviation and finds it is $6.09. Using these values, he determines the sampling error of the mean as:

$$E_y = ts/ \sqrt{n} = (1.96)(6.09) / \sqrt{100} = \$1.19$$

The sampling error of the cumulative costs for supplies of all 1000 requisitions would be:

$$1000 \text{ x } 1.19 = \$1190$$

Therefore, the estimated cost spent on supply requisitions would be the calculated average of the sample, multiplied by the population, give or take $1190 due to sampling error.

Copyright © Mometrix Media. You have been licensed one copy of this document for personal use only. Any other reproduction or redistribution is strictly prohibited. All rights reserved.

Adjusting Sampling Size

To adjust the sample size, the following formula is used:

Sample size (n) = (t-value)² x (standard deviation(s))² / (tolerable error of the mean (E))²

Example: From a population of 1000 supply requisition forms, the auditor samples 100 of them to estimate the amount spent on supplies in a year. At a 95% confidence level (1.96 t-value), he determines the sampling error of the mean is $1.19. He decides he would like to have a 99% confidence level (2.58 t-value) for his results and an error tolerance of only $0.90 from the mean, not $1.19. To determine the sample size necessary to have these more precise results, he uses the formula:

$$n = t^2s^2 / E^2 = (2.58)^2 (6.09)^2 / (0.90)^2 = 305$$

His original sample size of 100 forms would need to increase by 205 forms (total 305 forms) to have a 99% confidence level and to have a sampling error of plus or minus $0.90 from the mean.

Discovery Sampling

Discovery sampling includes a predetermined probability of having at least one rare occurrence in a population. This type of sampling is typically an investigative technique to detect avoidance of internal controls or fraud, such as fraudulent insurance claims or fictitious employees on payroll, and is commonly used in financial audits. To begin, the auditor must determine the intolerable rate of error, abuse, or fraud, and also the probability of finding one such occurrence in the sample, which is one minus the confidence level. Using this information, the correct sample size can be determined by looking it up in the appropriate table. The random sample should be scrutinized until an error, abuse, or fraud is found. If none are found, the auditor may state that the particular deficiency's rate of occurrence is less than the specified rate of intolerance.

Monetary Unit Sampling

Monetary unit sampling, also known as probability-proportional-to-size (PPS) sampling or dollar-unit sampling, is used for substantive audit testing when the unknown variable is proportional to an independent variable within a cluster. It is best used for testing or in estimating overstatements of account balances. Example: An auditor wants to estimate the dollar value an airline spends on baggage loss claims paid at the branch level. Since the variable (estimated dollar value) is correlated to the number of claims paid, he uses the monetary unit sampling method because it yields a smaller sampling error than other methods. The auditor assigns a number to each claim, keeping track of the range of assigned numbers per branch office. He then randomly selects claims, taking note of their respective branches. Because monetary unit sampling does sampling with replacement, any duplicate numbers that have been randomly selected are not eliminated. The monetary unit sample method allows each branch office, regardless of size, to have the probability of being selected proportional to the number of baggage loss claims it paid.

Non-Statistical Sample Selection Methods

Non-statistical sample selection methods require subjective decision-making on the part of the auditor. Such methods include: haphazard selection, block selection, and judgment selection. Haphazard selection involves randomly selecting a few items for a sample. Block selection uses a block of transactions or documents, such as a month's invoices or the last one hundred customer orders, to create a sample. In judgment selection, an auditor picks a sample based on his knowledge about the population, thus using his own judgment. For example, the auditor may send questionnaires on customer satisfaction to only long-term customers.

Copyright © Mometrix Media. You have been licensed one copy of this document for personal use only. Any other reproduction or redistribution is strictly prohibited. All rights reserved.

Stratified Sampling

Stratified sampling may be applied statistically, measuring the variation as a standard deviation, or may be applied non-statistically, measuring the variation qualitatively. This method divides the population into two or more parts, or strata, from which samples are randomly selected. For example, an entire population of invoices may be divided into strata based on amounts due; whereby those with outstanding balances of $0-$50 are in one stratum, $50-$100 are in another, and those over $100 make up the last stratum. The random selection within each stratum would constitute the population's sample. This method is used for: obtaining better precision in the sample selection, having comparative results for each grouping, selecting a larger portion of the sample from a particular strata (i.e., a grouping with a higher error potential), or acquiring a sampling from a population which exists among many locations. Sampling units may be proportionally selected from each stratum or disproportionately chosen, according to the auditor's judgment or a statistical formula.

Statistical Sampling

Sampling allows auditors to test a small sample of a large population in order to draw conclusions about the population in a cost effective way. There are two methods of sampling: statistical and non-statistical. When auditors use statistical sampling, they must use their professional judgment in the following activities:

- Determining what information is needed for forming an opinion and which testing methods should be used to get it.
- Defining a population by size and qualifying characteristics.
- Selecting a sample. Prior audit reports and internal control assessments help determine which records are more likely to have errors and are in greater need of testing.
- Determining the probability that each member of a sample is truly representative of the population, thus forming the level of confidence.
- Defining an error and the maximum acceptable error rate.
- Using the sample results to draw conclusions about the population.

Both, statistical and non-statistical sampling, follow the same basic audit procedures and require an auditor's professional judgment. The statistical approach uses a larger sample, mathematically configured; requires a computer; and provides objective conclusions. It only works with a few sample selection methods and requires technical training. It's sampling risk, the risk that the sample does not accurately represent the population, is measurable. The non-statistical approach uses a smaller sample based on judgment, does not require a computer, and provides subjective conclusions. It works with many sample selection methods and only requires minimal training. Its sampling risk is not measurable.

Tolerance for Errors

An auditor must determine the amount of sample errors that is tolerable and yet still renders useful results. For example, he may estimate that 3% of the sample records contain errors, give or take 1%. The auditor's determined level of tolerance, or desired precision, is the plus or minus 1%. The less precise the auditor needs to be, such as changing from a 1% to a 3% precision interval, the smaller the required sample size. The auditor's desired confidence level also affects the sample size. If he stipulated a 96% confidence level in the sample results that would mean 96 out of 100 sample results accurately represent the population within a specified amount. The greater the desired confidence level, the larger the sample size must be. In general, the larger the sample size, the more accurate the results will be. Therefore, a larger sample size is needed when the precision

Copyright © Mometrix Media. You have been licensed one copy of this document for personal use only. Any other reproduction or redistribution is strictly prohibited. All rights reserved.

and confidence level must be high while a smaller sample size is sufficed when the precision and confidence level may be low.

Calculating

The following set of numbers will be used to exemplify each of the definitions:

$$3, 3, 4, 6, 9$$

Mean: The average value among a set of data. It is calculated by adding all the numbers of a set and dividing by the number of values in the set. For example, the mean for the above set of numbers would be calculated as:

$$\text{Mean} = (3 + 3 + 4 + 6 + 9)/5 = 25/5 = 5$$

Deviation: The difference between one number in a set and the set's mean. For example, the deviation of the last observation in the above set of numbers (9) is:

$$\text{Deviation} = 9 - 5 = 4$$

Variance: The average of squared deviations in a set of numbers. The variance for the above set of numbers is:

$$\text{Variance} = [(5\text{-}3)^2 + (5\text{-}3)^2 + (5\text{-}4)^2 + (6\text{-}5)^2 + (9\text{-}5)^2] \,/\, 5 = (4 + 4 + 1 + 1 + 16) \,/\, 5 = 5.2$$

Median, Mode, and Range

The following set of numbers will be used to exemplify each of the definitions:

$$3, 3, 4, 6, 9$$

Median: The middle number in a set of ordered numbers is the median. When there is no middle number, the middle two numbers are averaged to determine the median.

$$\text{Set of numbers: } 3, 3, 4, 6, 9$$

$$\text{Median} = 4$$

Mode: The value most frequently observed within the set. In the above mentioned set of numbers, the mode is 3.

Range: A measure of distribution, calculated by subtracting the lowest value from the highest value. Based on the above set of numbers, the range is: $9\text{-}3 = 6$

Other Estimation Techniques

Ratio estimation yields more precise estimates than the basic estimation techniques of attribute and variable sampling. This is due to the sampling error being reduced by the positive correlation between the dependent and independent variables used in the ratio's calculation. The formula for ratio estimation is:

$$\text{Ratio Estimation} = \text{Dependent Variable} / \text{Independent Variable}$$

For example: An auditor feels the firm may save money by using a new vendor. The prospective vendor's materials are of comparable quality, with many items offered at lower prices than the

Copyright © Mometrix Media. You have been licensed one copy of this document for personal use only. Any other reproduction or redistribution is strictly prohibited. All rights reserved.

current vendors'. Of a population of 300 raw material purchases, totaling $3,100,000, he uses a 95% confidence level to sample 30 purchases, totaling $300,000. He determines $36,000 could have been saved on the sample purchases. Therefore, the ratio estimation is: $36,000/$300,000 = 0.12. This means 12%, or $0.12 of every dollar could have been saved using the new vendor. The population's total amount may be multiplied by the ratio to determine an estimated savings on the total purchases: $3,100,000 x 0.12 = $372,000

Difference estimation is used to obtain a more precise auditor estimation from which a book value already exists. It is calculated by multiplying the difference of the sample's average estimated audit value and the average book value by the population size. If the number is lower than the population mean, it is added to the population's book value, adjusting the estimated results upward. If the number is higher than the population mean, it is subtracted from the population's book value, adjusting the estimated results downward. For example, suppose an auditor has the following information and uses the difference estimation to determine the estimated dollar amount on inventory population.

	Sample	Population
Number of Items	300	6000
Est. Audit Value	$330,000	?
Book Value	$300,000	$6,300,000

Difference   Population

Estimation = Book Value ± [(Sample's average audit value - Sample's average book value) x Population size] = $6,300,000 + [(($330,000/300) – ($300,000/300)) x 6000= $6,900,000

Mean-per-unit estimation is used to estimate values that are unknown or unreliable. It is calculated as:

Mean-per-unit estimation = (Sample audit value/Sample size) x Population size

For example, suppose an auditor is trying to figure the value of an acquired inventory of 2000 items, all of which have unreliable book values. From a sample of 100 items, he estimates their combined value as $14,000. Using this method of estimation, the value of the acquired inventory, all 2000 items, is: ($14,000/100) x 2000 = $28,000

Variations

To achieve continuous improvement upon processes, data is collected, analyzed, and measured. Any variation, or deviation, from the standard process must be reviewed to determine the cause so that it may be reduced. Otherwise, a variation may result in a lower quality product, or it may create higher production costs. There are four basic areas in which variations may exist:

1. Employees – There may be changes in their physical or emotional state.
2. Equipment - There may be changes in air temperature and/or humidity.
3. Material quality – There may be changes in size, coloring, durability, etc.
4. Environmental conditions – There may be changes in its condition as it ages.

The three types of causes of variation in a process are: common causes, uncommon causes, and structural causes. Common causes are small in nature and are due to the process' internal factors. Variations from common causes can be expected in a stable and predictable process. Examples include changes in: employee performance, raw material, and the complexity of work orders.

Copyright © Mometrix Media. You have been licensed one copy of this document for personal use only. Any other reproduction or redistribution is strictly prohibited. All rights reserved.

Uncommon causes, or assignable causes, are large in nature and not necessarily part of the process. They make the process unstable and unpredictable. Examples include new competition, new products, a new market, and equipment failure. Structural causes are a combination of common and uncommon causes that are due to internal and external factors which may or may not be a part of the process. Examples include sudden increases in sales due to seasonal sales or sudden increases in production due to high demand for a new product.

Ratio Analysis

The reasonableness of a firm's financial statement may be determined by comparing some of its key ratios to those from prior periods. The best ratios to use are the current ratio, quick ratio, and cash ratio. They are as follows:

- Current Ratio = Current Assets/ Current Liabilities
- Quick Ratio = (Current Assets – Inventories) / Current Liabilities
- Cash Ratio = Cash + Marketable Securities / Current Liabilities

Additional helpful ratios include: accounts receivable, turnover, days to collect receivables, inventory turnover, days to sell inventory, and days to convert inventory to cash.

Cash Flow Statement

Cash is the asset most often misappropriated. Therefore the cash flow statement, which identifies the origins and flow of operational funds, should be analyzed to evaluate the possibility of fraud. It should be reviewed, ensuring the data has logical relationships, such as a decrease in raw material purchases should have a correlating decrease in accounts payable. Also, the auditor may convert the income statement's reported "net income from operations" into "net cash from operations" to further analyze the cash flow components. The formula is as follows:

Net Income from Operations +

Depreciation

-Increase in Accounts Receivable

+Decrease in Inventory

+Increase in Accounts Payable

= Net Cash from Operations

Net Worth Analysis

A net worth analysis of someone suspected of fraudulently obtaining company funds may be used as circumstantial evidence against guilty parties. There are two approaches to a net worth analysis: asset method and expenditure method.

If the suspect has been putting the fraudulent funds into investments or acquiring other assets, the asset approach should be used. The formula is:

Assets (valued at cost) –

Liabilities = Net Worth

Copyright © Mometrix Media. You have been licensed one copy of this document for personal use only. Any other reproduction or redistribution is strictly prohibited. All rights reserved.

-Previous Year's Net Worth =

Net Worth Increase

Net Worth Increase +

Living Expenses =

Income –

Funds from Unknown Sources =

Funds from Unknown Sources

If funds from unknown sources are in the same ballpark as the amount of missing company funds, the analysis serves as strong circumstantial evidence.

A net worth analysis of someone suspected of fraudulently obtaining company funds may be used as circumstantial evidence against guilty parties. There are two approaches to a net worth analysis: asset method and expenditure method.

If the suspect has been spending the fraudulent funds on non-asset ventures, such as travel or entertainment, the expenditures method should be employed. The formula is:

Expenditures – Funds from Known Sources = Funds from Unknown Sources

Expenditures include bank deposits, travel and entertainment expenses, and loan and credit payments. If funds from unknown sources are in the same ballpark as the amount of missing company funds, the analysis serves as strong circumstantial evidence.

Testing Computer Data

Testing computer data during an audit may be done by:

Bypassing the Computer – There are two ways to manually test computer data:

1. Computer output is compared to physical records, inspections, or is verified with third parties. Also, an auditor may use common sense to review the output for reasonableness and completeness.
2. Source transactions are selected. An auditor manually processes them and compares the results to the computer's output.
3. Using the Computer – To develop a computer program to test computer data, the auditor first must determine what computer information is needed to meet audit objectives. He should use the computer system's data dictionary to find which data elements the computer program uses for calculating that information, as any errors in those contributing data elements may create errors in the final computation. The auditor's computer program should be designed to either detect elements that do not meet specified standards or to detect illogical data relationships.

System Control Audit Review File

System control audit review file (SCARF) is a method of collecting data by the use of embedded audit modules which are coded into the computer application program. Data which meets predetermined criteria is recorded for further evaluation while the program does its routine

- 93 -

Copyright © Mometrix Media. You have been licensed one copy of this document for personal use only. Any other reproduction or redistribution is strictly prohibited. All rights reserved.

processing. It is more cost-effective to have these audit modules placed in the program when the program is being designed. It is the auditor's responsibility to determine the criteria for data selection and the placement of collection points, typically where there is a higher likelihood of errors or security issues occurring. This method is commonly used to reveal unusual transactions.

Collecting Computer Data

Audit techniques for collecting computer data: Fourth-generation programming languages (4GLs) are user-friendly software that allows auditors to acquire data from online data files, consolidate various data records or files into one, and complete many of the functions available in traditional audit software. Although 4GLs may improve an auditor's productivity, they are not as comprehensive as traditional audit software and are best used as supplements only. Audit hooks are computer programs within an application program that detect unusual transactions. They are typically used in high-risk systems. Extended records technique eliminates the auditor's need to check numerous computer files to reconstruct the processing of a particular transaction. Instead, one or more computer programs are used to gather data for a complete transaction, including the data from all the computer application systems which contributed to its processing. This combined data is then stored into one computer record.

General Audit Software Packages

General audit software packages allow auditors to extract, analyze, and test the accuracy of computer systems' data files based on the auditor's criteria. Since it allows more computer records to be reviewed and in greater depth, fewer audit staff members are needed, thus saving the audit department's resources. General functions of the software include: verifying data fields; selecting transactions; choosing statistical samples; and compiling, comparing, and running various calculations on data from differing files.

There are a few disadvantages. While these software packages are a proficient tool for verifying the accuracy of data files, they are not designed for testing a computer application's program logic. Also, they may only be used on hardware that has a compatible operating system. Finally, it may not be possible to use them directly in a database environment where storage access is complex. However, there are alternative ways for accessing a database. The needed section of the database may be copied into a sequential file where it may be accessed by the audit software; or another approach would be to access the database using the database management system software via a created computer interface program.

Audit Software Tools

Programmers write a source code which identifies a program's capabilities. Any changes to a program must be done through its source code. Therefore, using a source code compare utility program is helpful for identifying any program changes, both authorized and unauthorized. It compares two versions of a source code, line by line, noting any additions, deletions, or changes. The auditor researches the supporting documentation around the identified changes, verifying the reasons and authorizations for them. For a more thorough examination of program changes, an object code compare utility program is used in conjunction with a source code compare utility program. Source code is translated into object code, a language readable by the machine. The object code compare utility software compares two versions of an object code and notes any differences. Using both the source code and object code compare tools, the auditor may verify that the program's object code is in agreement with the authorized source code and may adequately detect and research program changes.

Copyright © Mometrix Media. You have been licensed one copy of this document for personal use only. Any other reproduction or redistribution is strictly prohibited. All rights reserved.

Software

Automated Documentation software helps auditors with their fieldwork, as it is able to compare a program at two different points in time (as before and after a change), showing the results through flowcharts, tables, and graphs. Specific types of automated documentation software include:

- Automated Flowchart software is able to convert a computer program's source code into an easy-to-understand flowchart.
- Computer Data File Translation software formats a computer program's data file descriptions into a table or graph.
- Job Control Language software graphs or charts the sequential steps of the job control flow.
- Terminal Audit software allows a remote terminal to directly access data files from online databases. It is capable of the same basic functions as the general audit software, which is used with batch data.
- Spreadsheet Audit software's functions include: revealing cell contents, verifying logic through the documentation of macros, and creating an overview of the spreadsheet application's contents. Training is needed for using this software.
- File Comparison Utility programs are tools created and offered by software vendors for companies to run data file comparisons. The utility program detects differing values or names in data fields of two different files. For example, it may be used to verify an account file, such as Accounts Payable, has a matching total in the general ledger file.

Test Data Method

The Test Data Method uses test cases that have already had the results of the data manually calculated. The test data is "fed" into the program being tested. Once it is processed, the results are compared to the expected results. Any discrepancies are further investigated. This method is useful for testing batch or online programs. It is meant for evaluating a computer program's logic, not for verifying the accuracy of its data files. The test data method may be coupled with an automated code optimizer program to obtain a report on the frequency with which line codes are executed, thus showing areas of the program that are not used during processing.

Computer Application Evaluation

Computer application evaluation techniques:

- Base Case System Evaluation (BCSE) – System users collaborate with auditors to create a body of data, including input, parameters, and output, which is used to serve as the standard base case in which the computer application system will correctly run. This technique is commonly used for validating production systems but may also be used for testing programs that are in development.
- Integrated Test Facility (ITF) – Using this technique, the auditor allows his test data to be processed with real production data. The processed results are then compared with the pre-calculated expected results. After testing, the fictitious test data must be removed from the real production files. This technique is for testing the logic and functions of computer application programs of batch or online systems.
- Parallel simulation – Real data is processed through a test program which simulates a real application system's logic and controls. Generalized audit software is used to create the simulated program. This method tests an application program's logic, procedures, and controls.

Copyright © Mometrix Media. You have been licensed one copy of this document for personal use only. Any other reproduction or redistribution is strictly prohibited. All rights reserved.

Snapshot Audit Tool

The snapshot tool helps an auditor understand a computer program's decision-making process by taking a "snapshot" of the computer memory's parts that contain the data elements which were used in the decision-making process of a specific decision. An audit log file tracks input transactions; records the date, time, and placement of where in the program the snapshot was taken; and reports the results. When used with other audit methods, such as the integrated test facility, the results of various types of inputs can be foreseen. It is more cost-effective to add the necessary code for triggering a snapshot during the development of the application system.

Computer Audit Techniques

- Tracing – Tracing allows an auditor to follow a transaction's path through a program, as it shows the sequential instructions which were executed in the program while the transaction was being processed. From this information, the auditor may determine whether there is compliance with organizational policies and procedures.
- Mapping – This is a technique which uses software measurement tools to identify program logic not yet tested. Auditors use these software measurement tools to find unexecuted program statements to pinpoint programming inefficiencies.
- Control Reprocessing – An updated cycle of data is reprocessed. The results of the second processing are compared to the first results. This technique is used to identify records that are incomplete or lost.

Benchmarking

Benchmarking is about identifying and incorporating the best methods for performing business processes. First an organization must review its own major business processes. Next, it must obtain comparative data by attending trade conferences, studying publications, consulting industry experts, and researching customer and supplier opinions, among other methods. This data is used as a standard to measure the performance of the firm's current practices. Performance gaps between the two are noted so improved practices may be adopted where needed.

The two types of benchmarking are business process benchmarking and computer system benchmarking. Business process benchmarking focuses on the firm's processes, such as product design, marketing, and delivery methods. Computer system benchmarking is aimed at computer function procedures, such as acquiring computer hardware and software, designing computer systems, and system performance. The goal for both types of benchmarking is to improve processes and, at best, obtain a competitive advantage. There are six ways to benchmark. They are as follows:

- Internal Benchmarking – Management reviews its own processes. By identifying necessary activities, the activities with little or no value are more easily recognized and may be removed, thus streamlining operations.
- Competitive Benchmarking – Comparative data is compiled from researching the performance of direct competitors.
- Industry Benchmarking – Trends within the industry of the firm are studied and used as standards for comparative analysis.
- Best-in-Class Benchmarking – Practices among many industries are reviewed. The best ones serve as benchmarks so the firm may strive for achieving a competitive edge.

Copyright © Mometrix Media. You have been licensed one copy of this document for personal use only. Any other reproduction or redistribution is strictly prohibited. All rights reserved.

- Process Benchmarking – Particular processes, such as product distribution or employee hiring, are studied in companies with similar functions, regardless of their industry. The most efficient and effective processes are used for comparison.
- Strategic Benchmarking – The best competitive strategies are sought. Improvements in this area should bring increased market share.

Interviews

There are two types of interviews: structured and unstructured. Structured interviews ask the same questions with the same possible responses to several individuals while unstructured interviews ask open-ended questions for unique interviews. All questions should be concise and use language that is clear and appropriate for the interviewee. If the questions are too complex or use unfamiliar acronyms or jargon, the interviewee may not answer or just guess at the meaning and possibly answer incorrectly. On the flipside, if questions are oversimplified, the interviewee may feel the interviewer is being condescending, thus damaging the rapport and lessening the care of how they answer. Also questions and the choice of responses should be free from bias so that the interviewees are not influenced, but rather express their true feelings on issues. And finally, questions should be asked in a logical order, such as chronologically or grouped by topic. Questions that allow the interviewer (auditor) to establish a rapport with the interviewee (auditee) should be asked early.

Role

To help establish a rapport with the interviewee, the auditor should dress similarly, such as wear a suit while interviewing a formal manager or dress casually while questioning an employee from an assembly line. By giving participants a general idea of how long the interview will take, auditors are indirectly acknowledging the extra time and effort interviewees are giving, which further develops the rapport. Next, explaining the importance of the interviewee's responses will encourage thorough and sincere answers. While asking the questions, it is important for the auditor to use a calm voice, free from inflection, so as to avoid emphasis on particular words that could make the question biased. Facial expressions and body language should show little emotion so that the interviewee does not feel judged or rushed. If the answer given seems inconsistent, the auditor may repeat the question. If the answer is too vague to be a sufficient answer, the auditor may probe using neutral questions, such as, "What do you mean?" or "Can you elaborate on that?"

Interviews or Questionnaires

The following factors should be considered when deciding between doing interviews and using questionnaires: staffing, facility availability, time restrictions, costs, and the type of information needed. Since face-to-face interviews typically last an hour, more questions may be asked than in a telephone interview, which should be no more than 30 minutes. Advantages to the face-to-face interview are that more complex questions may be asked, and also body language may be observed and recorded along with the verbal responses.

Mail questionnaires are good when the information needed is easy for the respondents to answer. If it is too involved or requiring minute details, respondents may not recall or know the answers and either not respond or respond inappropriately. They are also good to use when the population of respondents is: large, located in different areas, and desiring anonymity.

A questionnaire may use open-ended questions or closed-ended questions. Open-ended questions elicit free responses, making it more difficult to interpret their answers and tabulate the results. Since these questions take longer to answer, fewer people may participate. This style works well

- 97 -

Copyright © Mometrix Media. You have been licensed one copy of this document for personal use only. Any other reproduction or redistribution is strictly prohibited. All rights reserved.

for preliminary studies in an area or for formulating appropriate choices for closed-ended questions.

Closed-ended questions include yes/no, multiple-choice, or fill-in-the-blank type questions. Yes/no questions are for determining the presence or absence of a trait.

Multiple-choice questions usually have four or five choices including the last option of "Other, please specify". Fill-in-the-blank questions are usually used for gathering quantitative data. The desired unit of measure is typically expressed in parentheses following the blank. The results to closed-ended questions are easy to understand and tabulate.

Yes/No Questions

While creating yes/no questions, auditors must be careful not to write "double-barreled" questions, such as "Did you receive training and appropriate materials?" This is asking two things which the respondent may not be able to answer if each part of the question yields different results (i.e., yes, they received training, but no, they did not receive materials). Also, questions using a negative should be avoided. For example, answering, yes or no to: "Does your department not log complaints?" would be confusing.

An expanded yes/no format includes more choices to show the degree of yes or no. For example, the format may include a middle category of "undecided" for those who are not committed to a "yes" or "no" or an escape choice, such as "not applicable" for those answering a question that does not pertain to them. These extra choices free the respondent from the strict "yes" or "no" options, allowing the results to be more accurate.

Quality

It is important to ensure a questionnaire is able to communicate effectively so that each member of the target population will interpret the material correctly. The following methods may be used during the design phase to assure the quality of a questionnaire:

- Pretest – A sample of respondents, representative of the population, are observed as they complete the questionnaire. Afterwards they are briefly asked for their opinions of the questionnaire so that misunderstood or difficult questions may be identified and either improved or dropped.
- Expert Review – Audit managers, auditee managers, or business professors familiar with the topic and respondents are examples of experts which may critique the questionnaire to determine if the questions will obtain the information necessary for the audit and whether the target population will have the knowledge for answering those types of questions.
- Peer Review – Other auditors may contribute their input.

Techniques for Quality Assurance

During the data collection and analysis phases, a questionnaire's data may be:

- Validated – This refers to making sure a questionnaire truly measures the variables it is supposed to measure, thus giving the auditor appropriate data to draw conclusions and make recommendations. This may be accomplished by studying the relationship between factors, ensuring they are appropriately correlated, either negatively or positively.
- Verification – This involves comparing a sampling of the questionnaire's answers to documents, records, or on-site observations. How much verification needs to be done depends on the data's importance to the audit, its likelihood of having errors, as well as, the time, resources, and available options for verifying the answers.

Copyright © Mometrix Media. You have been licensed one copy of this document for personal use only. Any other reproduction or redistribution is strictly prohibited. All rights reserved.

- Corroboration - Corroborating the results with an independent source of similar information is another technique for testing the data's accuracy.
- Reliability – This means ensuring a questionnaire's results will be the same by repeating the test, under similar circumstances, to the same respondents.

Ranking

Questionnaires may direct respondents to rank the importance of issues or items relative to one another by assigning values to them. For example, they may be asked to rank the six causes of reduced productivity, with 1 being the biggest contributing factor and 6 being the smallest contributing factor. This may help auditors understand what issues concern the auditee most, allowing them insight into where they need to probe further. For reliable results, it is best to have no more than 7 categories. Also, the instructions must be clear to alleviate the risk of respondents ranking the items in reverse order, omitting an item from being ranked, or assigning the same value to two items.

Rating Items

Rating questions ask for an item to be rated, using one of the available choices. For example they may ask: "How would you rate the effectiveness of the operational process?" The choices offered may be: "highly effective", "somewhat effective", "barely effective", and "not effective". A variation of this is the Likert Scale whereby an opinion on an issue is asked and given these choices: "strongly agree", "agree more than disagree", "undecided", "disagree more than agree", "strongly disagree". A rating scale may also be given to collect data on frequencies or occurrences. For example, if the respondent is asked how often they use the support staff, the choices given may be: "rarely, if ever"; "sometimes"; "frequently"; "very frequently"; "always, or almost always". Rating questions are quick and easy to design and administer. They provide quantitative results, which are easy to analyze and compare. However, there is not much depth in this type of feedback.

Focus Groups

A focus group is a group interview with 6-12 people. An impartial moderator asks questions and facilitates the group's discussion. This method is beneficial during the survey phase; it allows the auditor to acquire background information, identify potential problems, and obtain the auditees' general opinions on issues, policies, and products. The advantages of focus groups are that they are a quick and inexpensive method for obtaining qualitative data; the members are able to react and expand on other members' responses; and there is a direct interaction between the moderator and respondents. This interaction allows opportunities for the moderator to observe nonverbal responses, clarify answers, and ask follow-up questions. Likewise, it allows the respondents a chance to explain the reasoning behind their responses. A disadvantage to focus groups is that their results are difficult to summarize and tabulate since they are open-ended responses. Also, the results may be biased if the group had a highly-opinionated individual with a domineering personality. Meanwhile a group of reserved individuals may not be forthcoming with their responses.

Copyright © Mometrix Media. You have been licensed one copy of this document for personal use only. Any other reproduction or redistribution is strictly prohibited. All rights reserved.

Process Maps

Process maps are useful for giving new employees an overview of the organization's major procedures, as well as, an understanding of their specific role, as these maps help clarify employee involvement. They are also used to organize work and to pinpoint inefficiencies.

- Cross-Functional Process Maps – These diagrams show the sequence of steps within an organization's major work processes, and how they involve the various business functions.
- Relationship Maps – These documents explain the types of relationships which exist among the major business functions and how the functions interact with one another.
- Flowcharts – They diagram a process and are usually supplemented by supporting documentation. For complex systems, it is best to create a summary flowchart to serve as an overview of the whole system, and a detailed flowchart to assist in evaluating and testing internal controls. Vertical flowcharts simply show a process' steps. Horizontally-drawn flowcharts, which are more common, additionally include the interacting department's involvement in the process.

Control Charts

A control chart is a statistical tool used to improve a process' quality by distinguishing its common variations from its uncommon ones and measuring variations in quality. There are two types of control charts: attribute and variable charts. Variable control charts are used to improve process performance by showing variations in the quality of measured characteristics. Such measurements may include: time, height, length, width, weight, and temperature. There are several types of variable control charts. The more popular ones include:

- X Bar Chart – shows variation in the sample's average value.
- R Chart – records the sample's range of values
- S Chart – measures the sample's standard deviation.
- Median Chart – records the middle value of the sample's ordered observations.

An <u>attribute control chart</u> records product quality based on whether certain measurable characteristics, such as dents, missing pieces, and color, either conform or do not conform to standards. Nonconformities, or the quality characteristics, which deviate from specified standards, are charted, as well as, nonconforming units, which are the products/services containing one or more nonconformity. There are two charts for nonconformities. The c chart has a discrete scale displaying the number count of nonconformities in a fixed unit while the u chart has a continuous scale showing the count of nonconformities in a changeable unit. Both charts are based on the Poisson distribution. There are also two charts for nonconforming units. The proportion chart (p chart) displays the percentage or fraction of nonconforming units in a sample while a number proportion chart (np chart) shows the number of nonconforming units. These charts are based on binomially distributed counts. To calculate the proportion of nonconformities (p), the number of nonconforming units in the sample (np) is divided by the number of units in the sample (n), shown as:

$$p = np/n$$

Copyright © Mometrix Media. You have been licensed one copy of this document for personal use only. Any other reproduction or redistribution is strictly prohibited. All rights reserved.

Audits

Risk Factors

High-risk areas demand faster attention and so resources should be allocated to them first. An area of great concern is the quality of the internal control system. Its design and performance record are factors that determine the probability of weaknesses in the system. The greater the weaknesses, the more audit resources they require. Other factors that contribute to weaknesses and thus need more audit resources include: less competent management who inadvertently make poor decisions, questionable management integrity due to personalities or demanding pressures to improve performance that leads to fraudulent temptations, recent changes in systems or key personnel, high complexity of operations, a large or fast-growing audit unit, liquid assets that commonly attract criminal temptations, low employee morale, centralized computer processing with sensitive information in one location, and a considerable length of time since the last audit.

Risk Assessment

The judgment and intuition approach, or commonly known as the gut feeling approach, refers to the auditor assessing risk as high, medium, and low based on his professional experiences and education. The quantitative method figures the annual loss exposure (ALE) by multiplying the assessed impact cost of an adverse event happening (I) by the estimated frequency of the adverse event occurring in a given year (F). As an equation, it appears as:

$$\text{Annual Loss Exposure (ALE)} =$$

$$\text{Estimated Impact Cost (I)} \times \text{Estimated Yearly Frequency (F)}$$

Scoring Approach

The scoring approach considers various audit risks in an area and assigns them weight factors based on their level of importance, such as: quality of the internal control system 30%, audit unit size 20%, complexity of operations 20%, liquidity of assets 15%, and length of time since the last audit 15%. The weight factors may be determined using the Delphi technique. This is a method of trying to reach a consensus through a series of questionnaires, which in this case would be given to the audit staff. The next step in the scoring approach is to evaluate the risk level of each audit risk, "0" for a low risk level to "4" for a high risk level. Multiplying the weighted factor by the risk level determines the weighted risk score. Adding all of the weighted risk scores together provides the area risk score. Audits may be prioritized by comparing area risk scores.

Standardized Audit Programs

Developing a standardized audit program takes little time and requires minimal knowledge of operations in the audit unit. Consequently, it is easy for inexperienced auditors to follow. Standardized programs are best for operating environments with no or little change, for routine audits, or multiple locations with nearly identical operations. In contrast, customized audit programs require experienced auditors with a good amount of knowledge of the operations in order to develop an appropriate program. Naturally customized programs take more time to create. They are best-suited for complex or changing operating environments or unique audit circumstances.

Scope of an Audit

Determining the scope of an audit requires understanding the area, as well as, considering the needs of those who will be using the audit report, legalities affecting the audit unit, the internal control system, and other work recently performed by another auditor. Other things to factor in

- 101 -

Copyright © Mometrix Media. You have been licensed one copy of this document for personal use only. Any other reproduction or redistribution is strictly prohibited. All rights reserved.

include the criteria needed for evaluations, previous audit recommendations, and possible sources of reliable data. If unreasonable limitations are stifling the scope of the audit, such as unrealistic time constraints or management's restriction of certain sources, the director of internal auditing should inform the audit committee of these limitations and their possible effects.

Audit Evidence

Audit evidence is the information gathered through observation, interviews, records, documents, and test results for the purpose of providing a basis for an audit opinion. The four types of evidence are: physical, testimonial, documentary, and analytical. Testimonial evidence is the information gathered from interviews and questionnaires. The auditor must cautiously determine if it is accurate and unbiased. For this information to become an effective piece of evidence, it should be in the form of a signed, written statement.

Analytical evidence is obtained by calculating, comparing, and making logical deductions. An example, of analytical evidence would be the comparison of current expense accounts with the previous year's accounts to determine their reasonableness.

Physical audit evidence is obtained through inspecting and observing the audit environment. There are various means of documenting such evidence, including written reports, photographs, and actual samples. For example, an auditor may notice faulty wiring in an area of operations. A photograph of it provides evidence of the fire hazard.

Documentary audit evidence includes contracts, employee records, accounting records, invoices, receipts, and business letters. For instance, a contract signed by a manager and a supplier with the same last name (later proved to be a close relative) may be taken as evidence of noncompliance with company policies.

Assessing the Evidence

An auditor uses three criteria for determining the appropriateness of using such evidence to make and support conclusions. He must determine if it is sufficient, relevant, and competent. For evidence to be sufficient there should be an adequate amount of it to support the auditor's findings and it must be strong enough to persuade a prudent person to reach the same logical conclusions. To be relevant, evidence must have a logical connection to the audit findings. Evidence that has been reasonably validated and is reliable is considered competent.

Competency of Evidence

Certain evidence is more convincing than others. A general ranking of most persuasive to least persuasive follows: evidence obtained through physical inspection, documents obtained from external sources, auditor observations, and management's replies to auditor questions.

Competent evidence can be reasonably validated and is reliable. A few guidelines follow: evidence from a reliable external source is considered more competent than internal evidence since it is less likely to be corrupt or bias; a correlation exists between the effectiveness of management controls and the level of competency, whereby strong controls ensure more competent evidence than weak controls; and evidence that is obtained directly through the auditor's observations, inspections, and calculations is more competent than indirectly obtained evidence.

Sources of Evidence

Audit evidence will either be obtained directly from the auditor or indirectly obtained through the auditee, a third party, or a computer system. When the source of evidence is through the auditors' direct collection, sufficiency, relevance, and competence of the evidence is based on the

- 102 -

Copyright © Mometrix Media. You have been licensed one copy of this document for personal use only. Any other reproduction or redistribution is strictly prohibited. All rights reserved.

methodology used and the auditors' skill levels. Evidence gathered from a computer system does not need to be verified if the purpose of its inclusion in the report is to provide background information, and it has no significance to the auditor's results. It simply needs to be noted that no verification took place. If, however, the computer data is significant and does have a bearing on the auditor's results, its validity and reliability must be verified. This may be accomplished by testing the data, the controls over the system, or a combination of both. If another auditor has previously done such testing, his work may be used as verification.

Evidence from auditees, despite managerial or employee confirmation of its reliability, must be validated with other evidence. Directly testing the data, the effectiveness of data reliability controls, or some combination thereof would suffice. If, however, these tests show significant errors, the data may be deemed unreliable, in which case the auditor has three options: find other sources of evidence, adjust the audit objectives so as not to need the unreliable data, or include the data in the report, specifying its limitations while avoiding drawing conclusions from it.

Typically, there are no reasonable means for verifying the reliability of data from third parties. If the data is significant to the report, it should be included along with its limitations; but the auditor should avoid basing conclusions from it.

Scheduling an Audit

While scheduling an audit, the audit manager must maintain flexibility since various factors may affect the audit schedule; unusual circumstances, such as a merger, may cause the auditee to be unavailable for an audit. Also, audit staff members may unexpectedly resign or need a leave of absence. Having alternate plans ready, allows the audit manager to carry on efficiently despite unexpected interferences.

There are two approaches for assigning audit staff: team and pool. With the team approach, individuals are always assigned to the same particular areas so they may become proficient in those environments. With the pool approach, individuals may be placed anywhere for an audit, bringing a wider scope of experiences. Combining the two approaches, whereby new staff is placed into the pool and experienced auditors are placed as teams, has proven to be successful.

Finally, audit managers must turn complex audit projects into smaller tasks, making them easier to manage. Established management techniques include: program evaluation and review techniques (PERT), critical path methods (CPM), and periodic progress reports.

Exit Conference

After the audit findings are obtained, an exit conference is held. The assigned audit members, audit manager, audit director, the operation's management, and those authorized to implement corrective action all attend. The purpose is to discuss the audit findings, to ensure there are no misunderstandings, to resolve disputed issues, and to come to an agreement on corrective actions. Afterwards, the final audit report is written. If a disagreement occurs during the exit conference and no resolution is reached, the audit report should document both the audit findings and management's reasons for disputing such findings.

Supervision

Audit supervision is continuous from the planning stages through to the final audit report. The levels of experience among assigned auditors and the complexity of the project determine the amount of supervision needed. With more experienced auditors, the supervisor may provide a general outline of audit expectations, whereas with less experienced auditors, the supervisor may have to supply more details on how to gather and analyze the data. A supervisor should

- 103 -

Copyright © Mometrix Media. You have been licensed one copy of this document for personal use only. Any other reproduction or redistribution is strictly prohibited. All rights reserved.

continuously review the audit working papers to ensure the assigned auditors are collecting evidence that is sufficient, competent, and relevant.

Audit Objectives

Revenue Division

Audit objectives to be expected within an audit of the accounts receivable department of the revenue division include:

- Determining the credit policy's appropriateness by using the accounts receivable turnover rate as an indicator; a higher turnover rate reflects a conservative credit policy while a lower rate indicates a liberal credit policy.
- Ensuring accounts receivable has recorded actual sales.
- Determining if all cash sales are being recorded.
- Examining overdue accounts, determining their ability for collection, and reviewing the allowance for doubtful accounts.
- Verifying employee observance of the refund policy.
- Assessing controls over the handling of mailed-in payments.

Marketing Department

Audit objectives to be expected within an audit of the marketing department of the revenue division include:

- Evaluating the efficiency and effectiveness of the marketing department's organized structure.
- Analyzing the screening process for sales personnel.
- Ensuring proper training and supervision of sales people.
- Inspecting written agreements about employee commissions.
- Verifying commissions were properly earned, figured, and recorded.
- Determining the reasonableness of sales projections.
- Reviewing product lines, comparing expected with actual profit margins.
- Determining the reasonableness of advertising budgets.

Billing, Product Distribution, and Warranty Departments

Audit objectives to be expected within an audit of the billing, product distribution, and warranty departments of the revenue division include:

Billing Department

- Ensuring the adequacy of controls over customer order processing.
- Checking invoice accuracy, verifying them against merchandise shipments.
- Verifying proper investigations are done prior to authorizing customer credit limits.

Product Distribution Department

- Reviewing distribution methods to ensure they are timely and economical.
- Verifying the proper handling and recording of in-company transactions, such as supply requisition orders.

Copyright © Mometrix Media. You have been licensed one copy of this document for personal use only. Any other reproduction or redistribution is strictly prohibited. All rights reserved.

Warranty Department

- Reviewing the warranty reserve account for accuracy.

Purchasing Department

Audit objectives to be expected within an audit of the purchasing department of the expense division include:

- Determining the accuracy of methods used for forecasting product needs, which are used in purchase decisions.
- Ensuring authorization is required for initiating purchase orders.
- Reviewing controls to ensure inventories are obtained with adequate quality and at reasonable prices.
- Examining the vendor selection process and resulting contracts.
- Assessing the procedures followed for placing and canceling orders.
- Verifying competitive bids are obtained for purchases exceeding a specified price.

Payroll Department

Audit objectives to be expected within an audit of the payroll department of the expense division include:

- Ensuring all changes in payroll require authorization.
- Verifying procedures exist for ensuring hourly wages paid match hours worked.
- Reviewing records for the proper recording of paid holidays, vacations, sick days, or jury duty.
- Verifying payroll records are safely stored for the appropriate length of time for tax purposes.
- Assessing controls over travel expense reports.
- Testing the accuracy of proper withholdings for tax and benefit deductions.

Accounts Payable and Receiving Departments

Audit objectives to be expected within an audit of the accounts payable and receiving departments of the expense division include:

Accounts Payable

- Examining controls which ensure payments are only made for goods received, any prepayments are explained and recorded, and no duplicate payments are made.
- Reviewing accounting records for accuracy and timeliness.
- Ensuring overpayments, refunds, or business credits are properly recorded.

Receiving Department

- Reviewing the procedures and controls for receiving shipped goods to ensure merchandise is counted and inspected before accepting it.
- Inspecting storage facilities of goods received, ensuring adequate security.
- Assessing the efficiency of the receiving area's physical design, allowing for timely disbursements of merchandise or company supplies.

Copyright © Mometrix Media. You have been licensed one copy of this document for personal use only. Any other reproduction or redistribution is strictly prohibited. All rights reserved.

Inventory Department

Audit objectives to be expected within an audit of the inventory department of the production division include:

- Reviewing inventory control techniques to ensure the raw materials inventory and finished products inventory are at appropriate levels, able to meet demand without an excessive supply on-hand.
- Ensuring there is a separation of duties for recording and physically handling inventories.
- Verifying accurate records of materials, work-in-progress (WIP), and finished goods.
- Determining if methods used for disposing of obsolete inventory is the most economical. Obsolete inventory is that which has not moved within the last year. Disposal methods may include returning the items to the original supplier, selling them to other firms, altering the product to make it more desirable, or selling it at deep discounts.
- Ensuring write-offs and write-downs of obsolete items are authorized and correctly recorded.

Manufacturing Department

Audit objectives to be expected within an audit of the manufacturing department of the production division include:

- Assessing the efficiency of the production schedule (i.e., similar products are scheduled back-to-back, reducing setup time).
- Verifying production documents are up-to-date and complete, detailing each operation of the production process, including standard operating times, allowable wastages and downtimes.
- Determining if engineering change notices (ECN), which are notifications of changes to the production process, are properly authorized and controlled.
- Assessing the efficiency of disposing raw materials which have become obsolete as a result of an ECN.
- Observing operations to determine if they are following specified procedures.
- Comparing actual to expected times for machine setups, operations, and downtimes, and reviewing reasons for sitting idle.
- Checking the accuracy of production logs.

Quality Control Department

Audit objectives to be expected within an audit of the quality control department of the production division include:

- Reviewing vendor selection procedures and assessing the methods used for evaluating vendor performance.
- Ensuring quality inspections of raw materials, work-in-progress and finished goods are adequate and timely.
- Verifying that defective material reports contain the necessary information and are sent to the appropriate parties in a timely manner.
- Determining if additional costs resulting from defective materials are calculated and billed back to the vendors. These costs may include: production and shipping delays, product failures, extra equipment setups, and customer complaints.

Copyright © Mometrix Media. You have been licensed one copy of this document for personal use only. Any other reproduction or redistribution is strictly prohibited. All rights reserved.

Shipping Department

Audit objectives to be expected within an audit of the shipping department of the production division include:

- Assessing the efficiency of the department's floor plan for obtaining, packing, and loading finished goods in a timely fashion.
- Verifying an accurate log of shipments is maintained.
- Ensuring the flow of proper documents occurs in a timely manner. An example of proper document flow would be the sales department passing customer orders to the shipping department which would then pass the customer orders and matching shipping receipts to the billing department for invoice preparation.
- Analyzing the methods used for selecting a shipping carrier and determining if the selected provider is timely and cost-effective.
- Reviewing customer complaints of damaged, incomplete, or not received merchandise shipments and assessing the procedures and controls for handling and recording them.
- Determining if freight invoices are properly recorded and paid.

Fixed Assets Department

Audit objectives of the fixed assets department include:

- Verifying that requests for capital purchases follow the proper procedures for obtaining approval.
- Assessing the approval process by reviewing approved capital project proposals for completeness (the inclusion of estimated costs, resource needs, and time schedules); checking if other options were explored; and if the project was included in the annual budget.
- Reviewing post-completion projects to ensure they are done properly. Post-completion audits compare actual and estimated costs and benefits, explaining any significant variances.
- Ensuring existing controls adequately oversee construction-in-progress to maintain proper documentation, accounting records, and expenditures.
- Determining if sales, transfers, or retirements of fixed assets are properly handled and accurately accounted.
- Reviewing the property, plant, and equipment (PPE) accounting records to ensure shipping costs and labor costs contributed to a fixed asset's installation are included as part of the fixed asset's cost, and thus are capitalized, not expensed.
- Determining the appropriateness of the depreciation methods chosen and the accuracy of their recordings.

Plant Maintenance and Cost Accounting Departments

Audit objectives to be expected within an audit of the plant maintenance and cost accounting departments of the production division include:

Plant Maintenance Department

- Determining if equipment repair manuals are up-to-date and if a preventive plant maintenance program is followed.
- Reviewing the maintenance work order system to ensure jobs are scheduled effectively and costs are controlled.

Copyright © Mometrix Media. You have been licensed one copy of this document for personal use only. Any other reproduction or redistribution is strictly prohibited. All rights reserved.

Cost Accounting Department

- Determining the basis used to develop the following standards: material usage and costs, direct labor time and costs, and overhead costs from obtaining goods and services.
- Assessing the reasonableness of the standards related to materials, labor, and overhead by ensuring they promote efficiency while still being attainable.
- Determining whether labor and overhead costs were included in the computation of inventory costs.

Cash Management Department

Audit objectives to be expected within an audit of the cash management department of the treasury division include:

- Assessing the security over cash earnings and verifying timely cash deposits are made into the proper bank accounts.
- Determining the adequacy of physical and computer system controls over cash.
- Verifying the authorizations of cash transfers and the existence of controls over unauthorized electronic cash transfers.
- Determining if bank statements are reconciled and how discrepancies are corrected.
- Reviewing controls over petty cash disbursements to ensure procedures are followed for proper documentation, approvals, amounts, and periodic audits.

Debt Securities Department

Audit objectives to be expected within an audit of the debt securities department of the treasury division include:

- Verifying that issuances of debt securities have received proper authorization and do not exceed board of director limitations.
- Determining if principal and interest payments on debt instruments is accurate and timely.
- Checking accounting records to ensure accrued interest is calculated and recorded correctly.

Equity Department

Audit objectives to be expected within an audit of the equity department of the treasury division include:

- Ensuring authorized but un-issued stock certificates, treasury stock, and acquired securities resulting from a company take-over are safeguarded against theft, loss, and damage.
- Verifying stock transfers are done properly and records are updated daily.
- Determining if conversions of preferred securities and debentures into common stock are calculated, verified, issued, and recorded accurately.
- Reviewing controls over stock issues to ensure they are consistent with the board of director's resolutions and follow legal guidance.
- Examining the stock option plan, including eligibility requirements and qualifying employees, to ensure proper notifications were sent and proper procedures are followed when employees exercise their options.
- Ensuring the redemption of securities receives board approval and is accurately accounted.
- Determining whether dividend declarations are approved, correctly calculated, and accurately accounted.

Copyright © Mometrix Media. You have been licensed one copy of this document for personal use only. Any other reproduction or redistribution is strictly prohibited. All rights reserved.

Investment Department

Audit objectives to be expected within an audit of the investment department of the treasury division include:

- Verifying purchases and sales of investments have received approval from the board of directors and are properly recorded.
- Reviewing purchase agreements and ensuring the correct escrow amounts have been deposited with financial institutions that have adequate insurance coverage and receipts of the payments are held by the treasury department.
- Examining the notes receivable to verify they are properly accounted for, to ensure payments are timely, and to evaluate the ability to collect from those in default.
- Determining if the write-off of an investment was authorized and justified. Justification that an investment is worthless may be provided by appraisals, public notices of bankruptcy, and information reported in financial newspapers or business journals.

Dividend Issuance Department

Audit objectives to be expected within an audit of the dividend issuance department of the treasury division include:

- Ensuring adequacy of controls over the issuance of dividend checks, such as updated stockholder information, secured storage of blank dividend checks that are pre-numbered, and secured storage of the signature plate by someone other than the individual responsible for storing the checks or authorized to print them.
- Ensuring proper procedures are followed for undeliverable dividend checks whereby they are converted to cash; relevant information about the shareholder and dividend check is recorded; and the dividends are escheated to the appropriate governments according to their abandoned property laws.

Risk Management Department

Audit objectives to be expected within an audit of the risk management department of the treasury division include:

- Determining if necessary risk exposures have an appropriate amount of insurance coverage, not too little and not too much, as may be the case from overlapping coverage or double insurance. Double insurance happens when in addition to the company's insurance; third parties also provide insurance, such as with leased equipment which is covered by the owner or merchandise that is insured with shipping carriers.
- Evaluating selected types of coverage and their costs. Also determining if certain discounts could be taken advantage of, such as reduced rates for improved security systems.
- Verifying that additions or reductions in property are promptly reported to the insurance provider, and all policies are periodically reviewed.
- Ensuring procedures are followed to document losses; causes of loss are investigated; and insurance claims are filed.

Copyright © Mometrix Media. You have been licensed one copy of this document for personal use only. Any other reproduction or redistribution is strictly prohibited. All rights reserved.

Currency Exchange Department

Audit objectives to be expected within an audit of the currency exchange department of the treasury division include:

- Determining if foreign currency exchange transactions follow the directives of the treasury management and the board of directors.
- Ensuring periodic evaluation, review, and approval of banks providing foreign exchange transaction services are conducted by employees from other departments.
- Reviewing accounting records to ensure correct currency conversion rates are used, and accurate calculations of gains and losses are correctly reported.

Journaling and Consolidation Department

Audit objectives to be expected within an audit of the journaling and consolidation department of the financial reporting division include:

- Reviewing journal entries to ensure they comply with generally accepted accounting principles (GAAP), as well as, company policies and procedures.
- Checking journal entries involving accrual and depreciation calculations for accuracy and compliance with company policies.
- Assessing the adequacy of controls over the journal entry computer processing system.
- Verifying procedures exist to ensure accurate and timely processing of the general ledger, such as the assignment of due dates to each authorized individual in a department for needing their journal entries consolidated and posted into the general ledger system.
- Verifying preliminary general ledger trial balances are checked by authorized personnel for accuracy and reasonableness and determining if mistakes, unreasonable data, or suspected causes of out-of-balanced results are promptly reviewed and corrected.

Financial Statements Department

Audit objectives to be expected within an audit of the financial statements department of the financial reporting division include:

- Ensuring financial statements are issued on time, reflect the data from the final general ledger, and contain the necessary disclosures.
- Verifying the storage of retained financial documents is in a place safe from fire and theft for a time period necessary to meet government regulations and company polices.
- Examining the methods used to dispose of records to ensure sensitive data may not be captured from the remains.

Tax Department

Audit objectives to be expected within an audit of the tax department of the financial reporting division include:

- Reviewing the tax calendars to verify tax returns are filed and payments are made on time.
- Verifying gains and losses are properly categorized as either ordinary or capital, as they are handled differently.
- Analyzing tax minimizing strategies, such as moving facilities to a lower-taxed area or choosing a more advantageous method of depreciation.
- Determining all required tax adjustments are accurately recorded.
- Ensuring sales taxes are correctly figured and stated on invoices.

Copyright © Mometrix Media. You have been licensed one copy of this document for personal use only. Any other reproduction or redistribution is strictly prohibited. All rights reserved.

- Verifying payroll taxes are accurately calculated and filed.
- Determining if real estate taxes are paid on time.

Network Management System

Audit objectives in reviewing network management systems include:

- Identifying the type of network environment as: dial-up (connecting terminals from various locations), leased line (connecting terminals between two destinations), or microwave (transmitting data via satellite).
- Ensuring the following duties are segregated: application programming, systems programming, computer operations, data security, and the network control group.
- Assessing the volume of network traffic. If it is high, then the auditor should determine if network-balancing procedures are being used or if alternative methods of transmission are needed.
- Ensuring there are documented and tested recovery procedures for the network.
- Assessing network configuration procedures used when: the network is down, components are removed for repair, or nodes are added or withdrawn from the network.
- Assessing the network's security by verifying: access requires user IDs and passwords, abandoned terminals are automatically logged-off, and it is able to restrict usage.

System Utility Program

The audit objective in reviewing a system utility program is the assessment of the controls over it. Audit procedures for accomplishing this assessment include:

- Interviewing systems programmers and application programmers to gain knowledge of the existing controls.
- Verifying proper procedures are followed and documented for obtaining approval to use the system utility program, as access to these programs is restricted since they have the ability to override controls in the application operating systems.
- Ensuring access requires a separate password.
- Determining if the identity of utility programs is protected by renaming them with only a few authorized employees aware of the name change.

Local Area Network

The audit objectives, with regards to local area networks (LANs), are to assess the adequacy of the security and integrity controls over LANs. Audit procedures include:

- Interviewing the employee responsible for the everyday operation of the LAN system.
- Ensuring written procedures for operating the LAN system exist and are updated by a designated person.
- Verifying individual user IDs are given, and entered passwords are encrypted.
- Speaking with management to determine whether data records, data fields, databases, or program files require data encryption or other heightened security measures to protect them from unauthorized access.
- Ensuring the network operating system's security controls do the following: limit simultaneous connections, require passwords to be unique and periodically changed, have account expirations, disconnect inactive connections, lock-out users after several failed password attempts, and log main file server activities.
- Ensuring authorization to use the LAN system requires end-user management approval.

Copyright © Mometrix Media. You have been licensed one copy of this document for personal use only. Any other reproduction or redistribution is strictly prohibited. All rights reserved.

- Verifying an adequate audit trail exists.
- Ensuring the LAN administrator knows and correctly performs his duties.

Value-Added Network vs. Wide-Area Network

Whether auditing a value-added network (VAN) or wide-area network (WAN), the audit objective is the same – to ensure the network services are fulfilling the needs of the business.

Audit procedures for reviewing a VAN include:

- Ensuring adequate security controls over the services provided by the VAN, which include: electronic data interchange (EDI), dial-in services, and access to the internet.
- Determining if VAN services are properly used.
- Verifying the configuration of protocols for the network is correct.

Audit procedures for reviewing a WAN include:

- Ensuring physical, as well as, logical security controls adequately protect the WAN devices, which include bridges, repeaters, routers, and switches.
- Verifying the configuration of protocols used in the network is correct.

Network Changes

When reviewing network changes, the audit objectives are to assess the procedures for making changes to the network and evaluate the adequacy of the controls over the process. Audit procedures include:

- Reviewing a sampling of changes completed in the network's operating and management systems, the database system, and operating system.
- Determining what affects the changes had on the access control security systems software.
- Verifying changes are logged, tested, and approved.
- Assess how efficiently network change requests are handled by comparing change request dates with completion dates.

Security Controls Over Systems Software

Audit objectives for assessing the security controls over systems software include:

- Ensuring written policies and procedures for accessing and utilizing computer programs are made available.
- Assessing the adequacy of the access controls into the system's resource facilities, such as identification cards, thumb print identification, or password encryption.
- Determining if appropriate default options were selected in the library management systems software.
- Ensuring both source and object code program libraries are updated and controlled by the library management systems software, which should report any changes and save prior program versions.
- Making sure cataloging procedures disallow duplicate program names to exist within the libraries.
- Assessing each library's program changing procedure controls, designed to prevent incorrect program versions from being put into production.

Copyright © Mometrix Media. You have been licensed one copy of this document for personal use only. Any other reproduction or redistribution is strictly prohibited. All rights reserved.

- Evaluating the adequacy of security functions over critical application systems. These functions include: system backup, restart, rerun, and recovery.
- Testing the system to determine if it recognizes and "kicks out" unauthorized processing jobs.

Application Software

The audit objectives for assessing the security controls over application software include:

- Interviewing the head of the security administration function, such as the data security officer.
- Ensuring users have restricted access to application programs in production with the exception of maintenance programmers who are granted access to all application programs but only to the extent of their purpose, such as to read, write, execute, change, catalog, copy, or rename.
- Verifying the application system has a transaction log file.
- Ensuring public data entry, as from a check-out touch pad, a touch-tone phone, or automatic teller machine, is stored on mirrored disks, located in different places on separate magnetic media.
- Making sure hash totals of characters are periodically calculated and compared to ensure there are no unauthorized changes to production programs.
- Verifying the library management software, which is used when making changes to applications software, requires a password for access.

Data Communications Software

Audit objectives for assessing the security controls over data communications software include:

- Verifying connections between host computers and users require a four-step authentication procedure whereby the host computer identifies itself to a cryptographic device which reciprocates by identifying itself to the computer, and then the user identifies himself to the cryptographic device and the device identifies itself to the user.
- Making sure the telephone numbers of dial-up connections are confidential and regularly changed.
- Comparing inventory records with the actual inventory of data communications network notes, lines, and equipment.
- Inspecting physical security controls over data communications hardware.

Security Controls Over Data

The audit objectives for assessing security controls over data include: verifying the user profiles, which identify the IT staff and functional users authorized to access data files, is current; and ensuring: access controls over production libraries are adequate, restrictions are placed on critical or sensitive data files, system logging procedures are maintained, and audit trails are adequate.

Audit procedures include:

- Determining whether data is classified by its degree of criticalness.
- Determining on what basis access is authorized to production data sets, files, and programs, and who is in charge of granting it.
- Assessing the accuracy and completeness of the inventory records maintained by the tape librarian function by comparing them to the actual computer programs, data files, and documentation manuals.

Copyright © Mometrix Media. You have been licensed one copy of this document for personal use only. Any other reproduction or redistribution is strictly prohibited. All rights reserved.

- Verifying magnetic tape files have a regular cleaning and certification.
- Making sure tape files are externally labeled, accurately matching their contents.

Security Controls Over Computer Terminals

Audit objectives for assessing security controls over computer terminals include:

- Verifying the written policies and procedures for accessing VDU/CRT terminals and their use for data entry, retrieval, update, and print are current and adequate.
- Ensuring all security and access control violations are reported on a designated terminal or printer.
- Determining if the complexity of password algorithms is adequate.
- Verifying that terminals will become inactive after a specified number of failed attempts to sign-in.
- Making sure each terminal's available data corresponds to its user's authorization levels.
- Ensuring some means of authentication is used for terminals to identify themselves to the computer system.
- Assessing physical access controls to computer terminals.

Security Controls Over Computer Data

Audit objectives for assessing security controls over computer data include:

- Ensuring data files are retained for appropriate time periods in accordance with laws, regulations, and management policies. Job accounting and system logging data must be retained in detail for at least six months; thereafter, a summary version may be stored.
- Evaluating the rules over the editing of critical and sensitive data within a database system, and the database administrator's efficiency in resolving conflicts among users of the shared data.
- Verifying passwords are individualized, periodically changed, and removed for terminated employees.
- Making sure an electronic separation of duties exists whereby no single employee has complete control over all transaction activities, which include adding, changing, deleting, updating, inquiring, and retrieving data.
- Making sure production data is maintained in a separate data library from test data.

Assessing Firewalls

The audit objective for assessing firewalls is to determine if they are properly placed in the organization to provide the maximum possible protection. This is accomplished by:

- Studying the firewall configuration reports and analyzing the placement of firewalls.
- Knowing the different types of firewalls used and their advantages and disadvantages.
- Determining if the advantages are greater than the disadvantages.
- Evaluating the risks and exposures.

Physical Access

The audit objectives for assessing the controls over physical access into the computer center should include:

- Touring the computer center and sketching its layout.
- Checking for a receptionist or security guards at entrances who are trained to check employee IDs and to challenge those without authorization.

Copyright © Mometrix Media. You have been licensed one copy of this document for personal use only. Any other reproduction or redistribution is strictly prohibited. All rights reserved.

- Verifying a backup generator is available during power outages for electronically controlled access devices.
- Ensuring a visitor log is maintained which details who, when, and why the visitor accessed the computer center.
- Making sure locks, bolts, hinges, and overall construction adequately reduces the chances of a break-in.

Environmental Controls

The audit objectives for assessing the following environmental controls include:

- Dust/Debris Protection – Dust particles may damage the electrical circuits of computer equipment. Therefore, it is essential to keep the computer center immaculate. An auditor must assess the cleanliness of the area and ensure it has visible signs prohibiting smoking, eating, and drinking. He should check with maintenance to determine if trash receptacles are emptied outside the room to prevent their dust from getting into the air.
- Temperature and Humidity Controls – To safeguard the computer equipment and magnetic storing of data from excessive heat and humidity, the auditor should ensure the computer room has its own air conditioning system with the air intakes located in an unpolluted area above street level covered with protective screening. Temperatures and humidity readings may be taken as a surprise audit.
- Fire Prevention/Detection – The auditor may gather information from the computer center manager and building maintenance engineer to determine: the fire-resistance of the walls, ceiling, doors, and carpet, where smoke detectors are installed and how often they are tested, and the accessibility of the emergency power shutdown switch. He should ensure: carbon dioxide or halon fire extinguishers are accessible for electrical fires while water-type fire extinguishers are available for other fires; that they are tested and strategically placed; and personnel is trained on how to use them. An auditor must also make sure paper, toners, cleaners, and other combustible supplies are not stored in computer room. He should determine how frequently fire drills are practiced.
- Written Emergency Procedures – Auditors should verify the existence of written emergency procedures, as they are essential for referencing and training purposes to promote preparedness.
- Water Damage Prevention – A greater risk of water leakage exists in the computer center if steam or water pipes run overhead, the rooftop has a cooling system, or the roof is in poor condition. An auditor may check with the building maintenance engineer to inquire about these things. The auditor should also determine the water tightness of exterior doors and windows, as well as, the adequacy of drainage beneath the computer center's raised floor, and that of the floor directly above it, as well as, adjacent areas. He should ensure electrical boxes beneath the raised floor are kept as high above the slab as possible.
- Natural Disaster Preparedness – The auditor should consult with the building architect or maintenance engineer to assess the computer room's structural abilities to withstand natural disasters (i.e. hurricanes, tornadoes, and earthquakes). He may also inquire about how well grounded the building and computer equipment is for electrical storms.

Disaster Recovery

Auditors gather information from interviewing personnel and reviewing documented disaster recovery requirements, test plans, and maintenance procedures for keeping the plan updated with

Copyright © Mometrix Media. You have been licensed one copy of this document for personal use only. Any other reproduction or redistribution is strictly prohibited. All rights reserved.

changes being communicated to the appropriate people. The audit objective is to ensure the plans are adequate and complete. Adequacy may be assessed by:

- Performing or reviewing a risk analysis to determine which application systems and hardware are essential to maintain during a disaster.
- Ensuring that in the event of a disaster, the functional users' management has pre-planned procedures for maintaining critical business operations until a backup computer could take over during data center malfunctions or until facilities would be restored or relocated after a natural disaster.
- Reviewing and evaluating risk management's assessment reports and the insurance policy. It must be determined whether the insurance adequately covers business interruption from computer failure or hardware/software damage and the cost of restoring files. Also, the needs for third-party fraud insurance and fidelity insurance, which protects against employee theft, fraud, and embezzlement, should be assessed.

Database Management Systems Software

Audit objectives for review of the database management systems (DBMS) software include: ensuring it was installed correctly, assessing its controls over security and data integrity, and evaluating its overall performance. Audit procedures include:

- Verifying the Data Administrator (DA) reports directly to the data processing manager. The DA is responsible for maintaining: data requirements, access controls, and procedures for data storage, retrieval, file security, and backup and recovery.
- Ensuring a separation of duties whereby the Database Administrator (DBA), who must approve changes to the data dictionary, is not be allowed to write application programs, partake in systems programming, or operate the computer.
- Reviewing and verifying the testing of the DBA's written procedures on database recovery, both online and batch portions of the system, in the event database files encounter total or partial destruction.
- Evaluating the adequacy of the audit trail which the DBA should establish and document.

Data Dictionary

An auditor reviewing data dictionary (DD) systems software should determine if: controls are adequate, usage is proper, and the data reliable. Some audit objectives include:

- Interviewing functional users: to hear their problems or concerns with the DD system, to determine if the system is user-friendly, and to ensure the users are given adequate training.
- Selecting a sample of critical data to assess its adherence to data standards.
- Testing input controls by entering valid and invalid data and determining if the system correctly accepts or rejects it.
- Ensuring the data processing staff monitors DD system errors and takes prompt corrective actions.
- Making sure the system's backup is kept current and recovery procedures are documented.
- The objective of auditing data warehouse, data mart, and data mining techniques is to confirm they are being used effectively to acquire current, reliable information which will improve marketing and operational decision-making and fraud detection.

Copyright © Mometrix Media. You have been licensed one copy of this document for personal use only. Any other reproduction or redistribution is strictly prohibited. All rights reserved.

Data Entry and Output Error Handling

Audit objectives in review of the data entry and output error handling areas of IT operations include:

- Data entry (batch and online)
- Ensuring a separation of the following data-handling duties: origination, entering, processing, and distribution.
- Assessing data editing and validation controls and making sure employees are unable to override them.
- Determining if batch control totals of inputs and outputs are compared to verify data is complete and accurate.
- Making sure the application system automatically puts rejected data into a suspense file, recording the date and time, the user who entered the data, and an error code. Corrections should be approved by a supervisor before they are re-entered.
- Output error handling
- Determining if the department's control group maintains an error log and documented procedures for handling output errors.
- Verifying errors are promptly and adequately handled.
- Making sure end users receive immediate notification of any errors found in output documents/reports.

Report Reconciliation and Distribution

Audit objectives for review of IT operation's report reconciliation and distribution are as follows:

- Report reconciliation
- Ensuring the data control staff reconciles the report totals of processed transactions with input batch totals and also reviews the report for completeness prior to its distribution.
- Automated report distribution
- Verifying access to report distribution system data sets, program libraries, and utility programs is properly defined and restricted.
- Confirming users authorized to view the reports have actual business reasons for needing them.
- Manual report distribution
- Determining if report distribution lists are updated to ensure that only appropriate people receive the proper reports.
- Making sure the time-lag between production and delivery of reports is minimal.

IT Operations

Audit objectives for reviewing report retention and disposal and microfiche/microfilm records controls within IT operations include:

- Report retention and disposal
- Assessing the reasonableness of established retention periods for paper, electronic, and magnetic records for the purposes of: system backup/recovery, management, auditing, tax, legal, and regulatory.
- Determining if actual record retention is in compliance with established retention periods.
- Ensuring records, particularly critical or sensitive ones, are properly disposed, as by shredding, burning, or degaussing.
- Microfiche/microfilm records controls

Copyright © Mometrix Media. You have been licensed one copy of this document for personal use only. Any other reproduction or redistribution is strictly prohibited. All rights reserved.

- Ensuring the process of identifying and converting records into microfiche/microfilm is adequately done.
- Inspecting the quality and security of the microfiche storage room.
- Assessing the availability of and timeliness with which microfiche and microfilm may be retrieved by asking the data control staff to locate specific critical records from long ago.

Computer Job Scheduling

Audit objectives of computer job scheduling within IT operations include:

- Assessing the accuracy and completeness of computer job setups by reviewing the job run sheets of important application systems and determining if the job and step procedures were programmed in the job control library as directed and placed in the proper sequencing (some jobs are dependent upon prior completion of other jobs).
- Determining the adequacy of access controls.
- Assessing operating controls over job scheduling.
- Verifying job schedules are created for each operating shift at least a week in advance.
- Making sure job schedules are compared and reconciled with actual job executions to ensure completeness.
- Confirming job scheduling data sets are routinely backed up for disaster recovery purposes.
- Ensuring unique job requests are handled in a timely manner without interrupting regular jobs.

Moving Software Jobs into Production

Audit objectives for reviewing the procedures of moving software jobs into production within IT operations include:

- Understanding what the process entails.
- Moving application system development and maintenance jobs into production may simply require the software to be moved within a single CPU. If it is to be used in a distributed environment, the software would have to be placed into several CPUs. Finally, it may require being installed across a network, making the process more complicated and creating the need for increased controls.
- Inquiring whether the movement process is manual or automated. If it is manual, the auditor should assess the complexity of the software environment and determine the costs/benefits of automating.
- Reviewing the testing procedures for approving new or modified software to be placed into production. If they are inadequate, there may be more production failures, resulting in downtime, corrupt data, and reduced confidence in data processing by end users.

Computer Operations Within the IT Function

Audit objectives for reviewing the computer operations within the IT function include:

- Ensuring job run instructions are complete and understandable, particularly for critical jobs.
- Assessing the effectiveness of controls and the efficiency of procedures over the execution of production jobs.
- Determining if the appropriate options and parameters are selected within the system logging feature.

Copyright © Mometrix Media. You have been licensed one copy of this document for personal use only. Any other reproduction or redistribution is strictly prohibited. All rights reserved.

- Ensuring computer operations management regularly reviews the system console log to monitor operation activities. Regular review of the log may help management to identify problem areas, questionable occurrences, and possible methods for improvement.
- Making sure file backups are produced frequently enough. An auditor should assess whether full system backups may be occasionally replaced with incremental system backups, which back up only the changes made since the last backup, thus saving time.
- Verifying problems are logged and promptly corrected.
- Evaluating the cleanliness of the computer room.
- Comparing vendors' contractual agreements for hardware maintenance with actual maintenance logged.

Tape and Disk Management Systems

Tapes are typically used for backup purposes while disk media are used for day-to-day processing and storage. The audit objectives when reviewing the tape and disk management systems within the IT operation include:

- Verifying the physical inventory of tapes matches the data center's number of maintained tape files.
- Ensuring external labels correctly identify the tapes' contents.
- Confirming internal labels contain the following information:
- In the header (first) record: file name and ID number; volume serial number, reel number, and sequence number; file creation and expiration dates; blocking factor; record length (bytes); and record type, such as fixed or variable.
- In the trailer (last) record: end of file indicator; number of records; and control totals.
- Determining if tapes are being retained for appropriate time periods.
- Making sure the tape library's environmental controls, such as temperature and humidity, follow vendor recommendations.
- Ensuring access to disk media management systems is adequately controlled.

System Logging and the Help Desk

Audit objectives in review of system logging and the help desk areas of IT operations include:

- System logging
- Verifying appropriate system logs are maintained.
- Ensuring log files are secure so users may not modify the system logging records.
- Help desk
- Assessing whether the help desk staff is adequately trained.
- Evaluating problem logging, tracking, and resolution procedures.
- Determining if standard timelines are established for problem resolution.
- Verifying problems are documented with clear and complete descriptions.
- Making sure a current call list is available for routing problems to the appropriate support staff.

Software Licensing

When reviewing software licensing, the auditor's objective is to ensure the risk of legal suits against the organization is minimized, if not eliminated. This is done by reviewing and understanding the terms of software licenses, as well as, ensuring the organization has not only established software piracy policies, but it has also made employees aware of them.

Copyright © Mometrix Media. You have been licensed one copy of this document for personal use only. Any other reproduction or redistribution is strictly prohibited. All rights reserved.

When reviewing the Web infrastructure, the audit objective is to ensure Web management handles problems and adequately uses controls to minimize risks to the organization. This is done by:

- Reviewing performance issues and assessing the need for quicker response times, which routers with larger capacities or faster modems could achieve, and evaluating the need for faster Internet connections, which may be obtained by upgrading backbone links.
- Ensuring Web resources are protected from intruders by controls, such as Internet firewalls, encryption, and digital signatures.

Information System

An information system includes computer hardware; software; data entering, processing, storing, and reporting; users; the automated and manual procedures used within the system; and documentation of all those components. Information system controls are to safeguard the system from loss, errors, omissions, unauthorized access, and to recover from such occurrences.

Audit objectives of an information system's audit are to ensure the controls are able to adequately meet their objectives, IS resources are allocated efficiently and effectively for meeting the department's and company's goals, and information is available, accurate, and timely. The audit scope would include automated and manual systems, logs, reports, and documentation.

Information Technology Audit

An auditor may review the organizational structure of the information system, its systems' manuals, and documentation standards. He may also observe operations, interview employees, and disburse questionnaires. He may test key controls and analyze data using samplings or computer-assisted audit techniques (CAAT's).

Audit objectives during an IT audit of an operating system include:

- Ensuring systems software is properly administered with a separation of duties for systems programming, applications programming, database maintenance, data security, and computer operations.
- Determining if selection from the systems software's available options regarding parameters, commands, and controls is appropriate to the needs, tasks, and circumstances, respectively.
- Making sure systems programmers use test machines for testing new software, updated versions, and programming changes prior to installing them.
- Verifying software is installed and used correctly.
- Ensuring sensitive programs are put into a protected library with the volume table of contents (VTOC) in a separate data set. Such protection is administered by security systems software.

Consulting Engagement

Depending on the needs of an organization, an information technology (IT) consulting engagement may include providing services in system development, or the planning of computer capacity, IT strategies, or IT recovery and continuity methods.

Copyright © Mometrix Media. You have been licensed one copy of this document for personal use only. Any other reproduction or redistribution is strictly prohibited. All rights reserved.

During a system development consulting engagement, an internal auditor should do the following:

- Determine if a system development methodology exists. If it does, he must ensure it's correctly applied.
- Determine the need for developing a new system based on the number and types of user requests for system service.
- Ensure the feasibility report has reasonable time and cost estimates.
- Review the system design to determine if the controls will be adequate and if it will meet the users' needs.
- Make sure plans for system testing are adequate.
- Ensure the appropriate employees will be trained adequately for using the new system.

Logical Relationships

An auditor should look for logical relationships in the financial statements. For example, if sales are higher, he should expect accounts receivable and outbound freight expenses to increase too; if inventory has increased, so should the storage expense; and increased profits means greater operational cash flows. An illogical relationship should be investigated, as it probably is a misrepresentation due to error or fraud.

Vertical and horizontal analyses may be used to determine the reasonableness of a firm's financial statement when comparing it to those of prior periods. In vertical analysis of income statements, the financial data is compared in terms of percentages of net sales. In vertical analysis of balance sheets, the financial data is compared as percentages of total assets. As a supplement to ratio and vertical analyses, horizontal analysis focuses on individual statement items' percentage changes from year to year.

Fraud

There are two types of fraud. One type benefits the organization. Examples include paying off government officials, altering financial statements to show a greater profit margin, or tax fraud. The other type of fraud "hurts" an organization. Employees embezzling funds, falsifying expense reports, or accepting bribes are typical examples of this fraud. In both cases, those responsible for the fraudulent acts usually obtain a personal gain, either indirectly or directly. Creating and implementing a control system is the best defense against fraud, which is management's responsibility. The internal auditor's responsibility is to scrutinize the system. He must identify the methods used to monitor business activities, as well as, those used to protect company assets. These include company rules, required reports, managerial approvals, and various other means of control. Once identified, he must evaluate their effectiveness, and then make any necessary recommendations to improve the control system.

Fraud Investigation

An internal auditor should be aware of the possible types of fraud typical of an area he is auditing, as well as, deficiencies in the control system, allowing the fraud to escape detection. Any unauthorized transactions, unusual records or activities, or other indicators of possible fraud must be reviewed by the auditor for determining if they warrant further investigation. If so, he must report his findings and reasons to the board and management. After determining to what level the fraud most likely extends, the auditor must organize internal auditors and necessary professionals, who he deems competent and objective, to carry out the investigation. He must coordinate their efforts with a planned procedure for identifying the party who committed the fraud, their motives, and their means of accomplishing it. After the investigation, a final report of the findings,

Copyright © Mometrix Media. You have been licensed one copy of this document for personal use only. Any other reproduction or redistribution is strictly prohibited. All rights reserved.

conclusions, and recommended changes should be submitted for review by the board, management, and legal department.

Fraud

An internal auditor may discover evidence of fraud, mismanagement, illegal activities, practices that are harmful to employees, endangerment to public health and safety, or environmental destruction. These activities will have a negative impact upon one or more of the following: the organization, employees, investors, the public, and the environment. If the information becomes public, an even greater negative impact may result, putting the organization's reputation, market value, and earnings in jeopardy. Therefore, it is best for the auditor to use the proper chain of command in reporting such discoveries. He should discuss significant findings with the management that has the authority to correct the situation. If that management does not effectively resolve the problem, the chief audit executive should discuss it with senior management. If senior management does not resolve the issue satisfactorily, then the CAE and senior management must report their differing opinions to the audit committee. In some situations, such as discovery of fraudulent financial reporting, laws require auditors to immediately report their findings to the audit committee.

The main goal of a fraud investigation is to uncover who committed the fraud, as well as, why and how they did it. Among the various investigative methods, the strongest cases are built on witness testimonies with documentary evidence to support their claims.

Early in an investigation a suspect may be interviewed. The purpose of an interview is to gather information. Silence is an effective strategy used by an interviewer; it encourages the interviewee to talk more. Typically, an interviewee should be dominating the conversation while the interviewer listens, taking note of the suspect's non-verbal behaviors, or body language.

Later in the investigation when evidence strongly suggests guilt of a particular person, the suspect may be interrogated. An interrogation tries to elicit self-incriminating information from the suspect. Typically, the interviewer does most of the talking, as the suspect will deny allegations and will resist incriminating himself until he is convinced there is enough evidence against him. At which time, he may confess.

Controls to Stop Fraud

Establishing controls to prevent fraud is less expensive than the costs associated with conducting fraud investigations. Fraud preventive controls include implementing: company policies and procedures, a fraud reporting hotline, fraud-awareness training, and security controls.

Routine and surprise audits are controls that help detect fraud. Fraud may be detected in audits during testing (analyses, observations, calculations, interviews, and document examinations), checking computer files for duplicate billings or payments, using data query tools to browse a database for specific criteria, or applying data mining tools to detect unusual data patterns.

Computer system controls are used to prevent and detect computer-related fraud crimes, as well as, recover from them. Examples of computer preventive controls include those restricting access to computer files, terminals, and programs. Audit hooks are computer detective controls that are programmed into the system to flag transactions meeting predetermined criteria. In the event a computer fraud does occur, computer recovery controls help limit the resulting losses.

Copyright © Mometrix Media. You have been licensed one copy of this document for personal use only. Any other reproduction or redistribution is strictly prohibited. All rights reserved.

Alleged Fraud

When investigating an alleged fraud, the first step is to determine if the source making the allegation is credible and reliable. This may be accomplished by verifying that the source does not have hidden motives, such as revenge or jealousy; determining if their information is firsthand or if they are simply repeating what they have heard; and corroborating their information with other witnesses and/or documents. A written account of the allegations, along with documented evidence, should be gathered. And finally, all parties involved in the alleged fraud, including the suspected employee, should be interviewed to obtain their versions of the incident.

Examining Documents

A great deal of fraud occurs from altering, destroying, duplicating, or fabricating fictitious documents. Therefore, examining the documents of transactions is a necessary procedure for gathering fraud evidence. Transactions usually begin with a source document, such as an invoice or check, and leave a paper trail through the accounting records, such as entries in the general ledger, postings into individual accounts, and cumulative amounts in the financial statements. Investigating a value thought to be understated in the financial statements should begin by examining source documents and following the paper trail forward to the statements. An investigation of a value thought to be overstated in the financial statements should begin by examining the financial statements and following the paper trail backwards to the source documents.

Whistle-Blowing

Reporting adverse discoveries, such as evidence of fraud, mismanagement, illegal activities, practices that are harmful to employees, endangerment to public health and safety, or environmental destruction, to a company member outside the auditor's usual chain of command or to an authority outside of the organization would constitute "whistle-blowing". An auditor should only consider such action if he has already tried using the proper chain of command and a serious risk still remains. In this case, reporting to a high authority internally should be tried first, leaving the option of reporting to an outside authority as a last resort.

Differences Between Frauds

If assets have been stolen, the fraud may be shown as the following:

- Openly recorded on the books – This shows the transaction with the correct amount, but with a fraudulent purpose. For example, funds may be pocketed and fraudulently recorded as a duplicate payment. This type of fraud is the easiest to discover.
- Hidden on the books – The fraudulent transaction is hidden in a larger, legitimate entry. For example, an employee may record and pay a supplier an inflated payment from which he receives a kickback from the supplier.
- Off the books – There is no record of the fraudulent transaction. Examples include an employee pocketing some of the cash received from vending machine sales or an employee taking customer payments that were designated for paying off an account receivable that already has been written off as bad debt. An off-the-books fraud is the most difficult to discover.

A repeating fraud is one that continually happens after a single initiation, whereas a non-repeating fraud must be initiated each time. An example of a repeating fraud would be setting up a payroll account for a fictitious employee and collecting the paychecks that are continually generated. A non-repeating fraud would be a one-time occurrence, such as padding travel expenses to receive extra funds along with the reimbursement.

Copyright © Mometrix Media. You have been licensed one copy of this document for personal use only. Any other reproduction or redistribution is strictly prohibited. All rights reserved.

Most fraud involves conspiracy, which may be bona fide or pseudo-conspiracy. Bona fide conspiracy means all the participants are aware of the fraudulent activities. In pseudo-conspiracy, some participants are not aware of the fraudulent intent.

Risk Factors

Internal auditors should be aware of the following risk factors that increase the chances for fraud to occur:

- Inadequate controls
- Poor communication among senior management
- The company is in debt to its credit limit
- Accounting department is understaffed
- Despite higher accounts payable and receivable, income has decreased
- Numerous complaints or suits have been brought against the company
- An increased number of year-end adjusting journal entries
- Unmotivated employees
- Excessive inventory
- Lack of audit trails
- The above mentioned risk factors are business pressures and opportunities which may tempt certain employees to commit fraud. These types of factors should be recognizable to an auditor. Factors that may not be recognizable are those of a more personal nature, such as employees who are: in debt and desperate, seeking fast financial gains, or seeking revenge.

Management Fraud

Management fraud occurs when high-level managers use their authority to circumvent controls. It usually involves:

- Overstating revenues and/or understating expenses to show higher profits for the purpose of gaining a promotion, bonus, or other perk. Revenues may be overstated by recording the following as sales: fictitious sales, deals not yet finalized, consignments, and goods put into storage. Expenses may be understated by deferring them to the next accounting period, understating raw material purchases, or overstating ending inventories.
- Padding an expense account to pocket the extra funds.
- Overstating inventories so the cost of goods sold value appears lower and profits appear higher. Methods for fraudulently inflating inventories include the recording of: goods that are nonexistent or have already been sold, goods shipped to another site and double counted, or scrap metal counted as real inventory.

Employee Fraud

Embezzlement is when an employee fraudulently misappropriates an employer's property after it had been entrusted to him. Examples of embezzlement include making fictitious documents, such as invoices, time cards, and receipts for the purpose of gaining funds; "borrowing" today's revenue and replacing it with tomorrow's; pocketing cash sales before there is any record of the sale; and taking company assets.

Corruption may result when vendors, suppliers, or contractors are trying to gain a company's business and offer gifts, free trips, or pay-offs to the company's decision-makers. Such actions may entice employees to make decisions that are in their own best interest rather than the firm's.

Copyright © Mometrix Media. You have been licensed one copy of this document for personal use only. Any other reproduction or redistribution is strictly prohibited. All rights reserved.

Fraudulent Financial Reporting

The Treadway Commission recommends auditors use analytical procedures to detect fraudulent financial reporting, particularly in high-risk areas. Furthermore, they suggest the more experienced auditors help select the analytical methods of review and participate in evaluating the reasonableness of values used in the financial reports.

Three main analytical methods are trend analysis, ratio analysis, and modeling techniques. A trend analysis compares the current account balances to those of previous periods to determine their reasonableness. A ratio analysis looks for major departures from the typical ratios of two or more financial statement accounts from prior periods. If a departure is detected, the cause, which may be unusual circumstances, an error, or fraud, must be determined. The modeling technique determines the reasonableness of financial data by looking at related operational data. For example, operational data, such as the hours of operation and the average indoor temperature maintained, may be used to determine the reasonableness of utility expenses.

Terms

Definitions according to the International Standards for the Professional Practice of Internal Auditing glossary:

Internal Audit Activity: A department, division, team of consultants, or other practitioner(s) that provides independent, objective assurance and consulting services designed to add value and improve an organization's operations. The internal audit activity helps an organization accomplish its objectives by bringing a systematic, disciplined approach to evaluate and improve the effectiveness of risk management, control, and governance processes.

Assurance Services: An objective examination of evidence for the purpose of providing an independent assessment on risk management, control, or governance processes for the organization. Examples may include financial, performance, compliance, system security, and due diligence engagements.

Consulting Services: Advisory and related client service activities, the nature and scope of which are agreed with the client and which are intended to add value and improve an organization's governance, risk management, and control processes without the internal auditor assuming management responsibility. Examples include counsel, advice, facilitation and training.

Governance: The combination of processes and structures implemented by the board in order to inform, direct, manage and monitor the activities of the organization toward the achievement of its objectives.

Risk Management: The process to identify, assesses, manage, and control potential events or situations, to provide reasonable assurance regarding the achievement of the organization's objectives.

Control Processes: The policies, procedures, and activities that are part of a control framework, designed to ensure that risks are contained within the risk tolerances established by the risk management process."

Noncompliance: A breach of company policy, procedure, contract, law, regulation, or grant.

Copyright © Mometrix Media. You have been licensed one copy of this document for personal use only. Any other reproduction or redistribution is strictly prohibited. All rights reserved.

Error: Unintentional noncompliance with laws or regulations, including misstating or omitting material facts within financial statements.

Irregularity: Deliberate noncompliance with laws or regulations, including misstating or omitting material facts within financial statements.

Illegal Act: Refers to an unintentional or intentional act of noncompliance with a law or regulation.

Criminal Act: An illegal act that is punishable by imprisonment and other penalties, such as fines and corrective actions.

Civil Act: An illegal act that is punishable by fines and corrective actions, but not imprisonment.

Fraud: The illegal act of purposefully misrepresenting one's self to acquire something of value.

Abuse: Abuse of a law or regulation does not mean it is violated but rather the expected behavior that is implied from the law or regulation is disregarded.

Terminology Used in Sampling

Sampling Frame: Means of accessibility to a particular population, such as a printed list, computer file, or physical stack of documents.

Statistic: A calculated number based on one or more variables.

Finite Population Correction (FPC) Factor: A multiplier used to reduce the sampling error or the sampling size in large samples (at least 5% of the population's size).

Standard Deviation: The most common measure of the dispersion of values in a set around their mean. It is equivalent to the variance's square root.

Coefficient of Variation: A ratio showing the consistency of the data. It is calculated as follows:

$$\text{Coefficient of Variation} = \text{Standard Deviation} / \text{Mean}$$

Mean Absolute Deviation (MAD) – The difference between the mean and an individual value within the population.

Copyright © Mometrix Media. You have been licensed one copy of this document for personal use only. Any other reproduction or redistribution is strictly prohibited. All rights reserved.

How to Overcome Test Anxiety

Just the thought of taking a test is enough to make most people a little nervous. A test is an important event that can have a long-term impact on your future, so it's important to take it seriously and it's natural to feel anxious about performing well. But just because anxiety is normal, that doesn't mean that it's helpful in test taking, or that you should simply accept it as part of your life. Anxiety can have a variety of effects. These effects can be mild, like making you feel slightly nervous, or severe, like blocking your ability to focus or remember even a simple detail.

If you experience test anxiety—whether severe or mild—it's important to know how to beat it. To discover this, first you need to understand what causes test anxiety.

Causes of Test Anxiety

While we often think of anxiety as an uncontrollable emotional state, it can actually be caused by simple, practical things. One of the most common causes of test anxiety is that a person does not feel adequately prepared for their test. This feeling can be the result of many different issues such as poor study habits or lack of organization, but the most common culprit is time management. Starting to study too late, failing to organize your study time to cover all of the material, or being distracted while you study will mean that you're not well prepared for the test. This may lead to cramming the night before, which will cause you to be physically and mentally exhausted for the test. Poor time management also contributes to feelings of stress, fear, and hopelessness as you realize you are not well prepared but don't know what to do about it.

Other times, test anxiety is not related to your preparation for the test but comes from unresolved fear. This may be a past failure on a test, or poor performance on tests in general. It may come from comparing yourself to others who seem to be performing better or from the stress of living up to expectations. Anxiety may be driven by fears of the future—how failure on this test would affect your educational and career goals. These fears are often completely irrational, but they can still negatively impact your test performance.

> **Review Video:** <u>3 Reasons You Have Test Anxiety</u>
> Visit mometrix.com/academy and enter code: 428468

Copyright © Mometrix Media. You have been licensed one copy of this document for personal use only. Any other reproduction or redistribution is strictly prohibited. All rights reserved.

Elements of Test Anxiety

As mentioned earlier, test anxiety is considered to be an emotional state, but it has physical and mental components as well. Sometimes you may not even realize that you are suffering from test anxiety until you notice the physical symptoms. These can include trembling hands, rapid heartbeat, sweating, nausea, and tense muscles. Extreme anxiety may lead to fainting or vomiting. Obviously, any of these symptoms can have a negative impact on testing. It is important to recognize them as soon as they begin to occur so that you can address the problem before it damages your performance.

> **Review Video:** 3 Ways to Tell You Have Test Anxiety
> Visit mometrix.com/academy and enter code: 927847

The mental components of test anxiety include trouble focusing and inability to remember learned information. During a test, your mind is on high alert, which can help you recall information and stay focused for an extended period of time. However, anxiety interferes with your mind's natural processes, causing you to blank out, even on the questions you know well. The strain of testing during anxiety makes it difficult to stay focused, especially on a test that may take several hours. Extreme anxiety can take a huge mental toll, making it difficult not only to recall test information but even to understand the test questions or pull your thoughts together.

> **Review Video:** How Test Anxiety Affects Memory
> Visit mometrix.com/academy and enter code: 609003

Effects of Test Anxiety

Test anxiety is like a disease—if left untreated, it will get progressively worse. Anxiety leads to poor performance, and this reinforces the feelings of fear and failure, which in turn lead to poor performances on subsequent tests. It can grow from a mild nervousness to a crippling condition. If allowed to progress, test anxiety can have a big impact on your schooling, and consequently on your future.

Test anxiety can spread to other parts of your life. Anxiety on tests can become anxiety in any stressful situation, and blanking on a test can turn into panicking in a job situation. But fortunately, you don't have to let anxiety rule your testing and determine your grades. There are a number of relatively simple steps you can take to move past anxiety and function normally on a test and in the rest of life.

> **Review Video:** How Test Anxiety Impacts Your Grades
> Visit mometrix.com/academy and enter code: 939819

Copyright © Mometrix Media. You have been licensed one copy of this document for personal use only. Any other reproduction or redistribution is strictly prohibited. All rights reserved.

Physical Steps for Beating Test Anxiety

While test anxiety is a serious problem, the good news is that it can be overcome. It doesn't have to control your ability to think and remember information. While it may take time, you can begin taking steps today to beat anxiety.

Just as your first hint that you may be struggling with anxiety comes from the physical symptoms, the first step to treating it is also physical. Rest is crucial for having a clear, strong mind. If you are tired, it is much easier to give in to anxiety. But if you establish good sleep habits, your body and mind will be ready to perform optimally, without the strain of exhaustion. Additionally, sleeping well helps you to retain information better, so you're more likely to recall the answers when you see the test questions.

Getting good sleep means more than going to bed on time. It's important to allow your brain time to relax. Take study breaks from time to time so it doesn't get overworked, and don't study right before bed. Take time to rest your mind before trying to rest your body, or you may find it difficult to fall asleep.

> **Review Video: The Importance of Sleep for Your Brain**
> Visit mometrix.com/academy and enter code: 319338

Along with sleep, other aspects of physical health are important in preparing for a test. Good nutrition is vital for good brain function. Sugary foods and drinks may give a burst of energy but this burst is followed by a crash, both physically and emotionally. Instead, fuel your body with protein and vitamin-rich foods.

Also, drink plenty of water. Dehydration can lead to headaches and exhaustion, especially if your brain is already under stress from the rigors of the test. Particularly if your test is a long one, drink water during the breaks. And if possible, take an energy-boosting snack to eat between sections.

> **Review Video: How Diet Can Affect your Mood**
> Visit mometrix.com/academy and enter code: 624317

Along with sleep and diet, a third important part of physical health is exercise. Maintaining a steady workout schedule is helpful, but even taking 5-minute study breaks to walk can help get your blood pumping faster and clear your head. Exercise also releases endorphins, which contribute to a positive feeling and can help combat test anxiety.

When you nurture your physical health, you are also contributing to your mental health. If your body is healthy, your mind is much more likely to be healthy as well. So take time to rest, nourish your body with healthy food and water, and get moving as much as possible. Taking these physical steps will make you stronger and more able to take the mental steps necessary to overcome test anxiety.

> **Review Video: How to Stay Healthy and Prevent Test Anxiety**
> Visit mometrix.com/academy and enter code: 877894

Copyright © Mometrix Media. You have been licensed one copy of this document for personal use only. Any other reproduction or redistribution is strictly prohibited. All rights reserved.

Mental Steps for Beating Test Anxiety

Working on the mental side of test anxiety can be more challenging, but as with the physical side, there are clear steps you can take to overcome it. As mentioned earlier, test anxiety often stems from lack of preparation, so the obvious solution is to prepare for the test. Effective studying may be the most important weapon you have for beating test anxiety, but you can and should employ several other mental tools to combat fear.

First, boost your confidence by reminding yourself of past success—tests or projects that you aced. If you're putting as much effort into preparing for this test as you did for those, there's no reason you should expect to fail here. Work hard to prepare; then trust your preparation.

Second, surround yourself with encouraging people. It can be helpful to find a study group, but be sure that the people you're around will encourage a positive attitude. If you spend time with others who are anxious or cynical, this will only contribute to your own anxiety. Look for others who are motivated to study hard from a desire to succeed, not from a fear of failure.

Third, reward yourself. A test is physically and mentally tiring, even without anxiety, and it can be helpful to have something to look forward to. Plan an activity following the test, regardless of the outcome, such as going to a movie or getting ice cream.

When you are taking the test, if you find yourself beginning to feel anxious, remind yourself that you know the material. Visualize successfully completing the test. Then take a few deep, relaxing breaths and return to it. Work through the questions carefully but with confidence, knowing that you are capable of succeeding.

Developing a healthy mental approach to test taking will also aid in other areas of life. Test anxiety affects more than just the actual test—it can be damaging to your mental health and even contribute to depression. It's important to beat test anxiety before it becomes a problem for more than testing.

> **Review Video: Test Anxiety and Depression**
> Visit mometrix.com/academy and enter code: 904704

Copyright © Mometrix Media. You have been licensed one copy of this document for personal use only. Any other reproduction or redistribution is strictly prohibited. All rights reserved.

Study Strategy

Being prepared for the test is necessary to combat anxiety, but what does being prepared look like? You may study for hours on end and still not feel prepared. What you need is a strategy for test prep. The next few pages outline our recommended steps to help you plan out and conquer the challenge of preparation.

Step 1: Scope Out the Test

Learn everything you can about the format (multiple choice, essay, etc.) and what will be on the test. Gather any study materials, course outlines, or sample exams that may be available. Not only will this help you to prepare, but knowing what to expect can help to alleviate test anxiety.

Step 2: Map Out the Material

Look through the textbook or study guide and make note of how many chapters or sections it has. Then divide these over the time you have. For example, if a book has 15 chapters and you have five days to study, you need to cover three chapters each day. Even better, if you have the time, leave an extra day at the end for overall review after you have gone through the material in depth.

If time is limited, you may need to prioritize the material. Look through it and make note of which sections you think you already have a good grasp on, and which need review. While you are studying, skim quickly through the familiar sections and take more time on the challenging parts. Write out your plan so you don't get lost as you go. Having a written plan also helps you feel more in control of the study, so anxiety is less likely to arise from feeling overwhelmed at the amount to cover.

Step 3: Gather Your Tools

Decide what study method works best for you. Do you prefer to highlight in the book as you study and then go back over the highlighted portions? Or do you type out notes of the important information? Or is it helpful to make flashcards that you can carry with you? Assemble the pens, index cards, highlighters, post-it notes, and any other materials you may need so you won't be distracted by getting up to find things while you study.

If you're having a hard time retaining the information or organizing your notes, experiment with different methods. For example, try color-coding by subject with colored pens, highlighters, or post-it notes. If you learn better by hearing, try recording yourself reading your notes so you can listen while in the car, working out, or simply sitting at your desk. Ask a friend to quiz you from your flashcards, or try teaching someone the material to solidify it in your mind.

Step 4: Create Your Environment

It's important to avoid distractions while you study. This includes both the obvious distractions like visitors and the subtle distractions like an uncomfortable chair (or a too-comfortable couch that makes you want to fall asleep). Set up the best study environment possible: good lighting and a comfortable work area. If background music helps you focus, you may want to turn it on, but otherwise keep the room quiet. If you are using a computer to take notes, be sure you don't have any other windows open, especially applications like social media, games, or anything else that could distract you. Silence your phone and turn off notifications. Be sure to keep water close by so you stay hydrated while you study (but avoid unhealthy drinks and snacks).

Copyright © Mometrix Media. You have been licensed one copy of this document for personal use only. Any other reproduction or redistribution is strictly prohibited. All rights reserved.

Also, take into account the best time of day to study. Are you freshest first thing in the morning? Try to set aside some time then to work through the material. Is your mind clearer in the afternoon or evening? Schedule your study session then. Another method is to study at the same time of day that you will take the test, so that your brain gets used to working on the material at that time and will be ready to focus at test time.

Step 5: Study!

Once you have done all the study preparation, it's time to settle into the actual studying. Sit down, take a few moments to settle your mind so you can focus, and begin to follow your study plan. Don't give in to distractions or let yourself procrastinate. This is your time to prepare so you'll be ready to fearlessly approach the test. Make the most of the time and stay focused.

Of course, you don't want to burn out. If you study too long you may find that you're not retaining the information very well. Take regular study breaks. For example, taking five minutes out of every hour to walk briskly, breathing deeply and swinging your arms, can help your mind stay fresh.

As you get to the end of each chapter or section, it's a good idea to do a quick review. Remind yourself of what you learned and work on any difficult parts. When you feel that you've mastered the material, move on to the next part. At the end of your study session, briefly skim through your notes again.

But while review is helpful, cramming last minute is NOT. If at all possible, work ahead so that you won't need to fit all your study into the last day. Cramming overloads your brain with more information than it can process and retain, and your tired mind may struggle to recall even previously learned information when it is overwhelmed with last-minute study. Also, the urgent nature of cramming and the stress placed on your brain contribute to anxiety. You'll be more likely to go to the test feeling unprepared and having trouble thinking clearly.

So don't cram, and don't stay up late before the test, even just to review your notes at a leisurely pace. Your brain needs rest more than it needs to go over the information again. In fact, plan to finish your studies by noon or early afternoon the day before the test. Give your brain the rest of the day to relax or focus on other things, and get a good night's sleep. Then you will be fresh for the test and better able to recall what you've studied.

Step 6: Take a practice test

Many courses offer sample tests, either online or in the study materials. This is an excellent resource to check whether you have mastered the material, as well as to prepare for the test format and environment.

Check the test format ahead of time: the number of questions, the type (multiple choice, free response, etc.), and the time limit. Then create a plan for working through them. For example, if you have 30 minutes to take a 60-question test, your limit is 30 seconds per question. Spend less time on the questions you know well so that you can take more time on the difficult ones.

If you have time to take several practice tests, take the first one open book, with no time limit. Work through the questions at your own pace and make sure you fully understand them. Gradually work up to taking a test under test conditions: sit at a desk with all study materials put away and set a timer. Pace yourself to make sure you finish the test with time to spare and go back to check your answers if you have time.

Copyright © Mometrix Media. You have been licensed one copy of this document for personal use only. Any other reproduction or redistribution is strictly prohibited. All rights reserved.

After each test, check your answers. On the questions you missed, be sure you understand why you missed them. Did you misread the question (tests can use tricky wording)? Did you forget the information? Or was it something you hadn't learned? Go back and study any shaky areas that the practice tests reveal.

Taking these tests not only helps with your grade, but also aids in combating test anxiety. If you're already used to the test conditions, you're less likely to worry about it, and working through tests until you're scoring well gives you a confidence boost. Go through the practice tests until you feel comfortable, and then you can go into the test knowing that you're ready for it.

Test Tips

On test day, you should be confident, knowing that you've prepared well and are ready to answer the questions. But aside from preparation, there are several test day strategies you can employ to maximize your performance.

First, as stated before, get a good night's sleep the night before the test (and for several nights before that, if possible). Go into the test with a fresh, alert mind rather than staying up late to study.

Try not to change too much about your normal routine on the day of the test. It's important to eat a nutritious breakfast, but if you normally don't eat breakfast at all, consider eating just a protein bar. If you're a coffee drinker, go ahead and have your normal coffee. Just make sure you time it so that the caffeine doesn't wear off right in the middle of your test. Avoid sugary beverages, and drink enough water to stay hydrated but not so much that you need a restroom break 10 minutes into the test. If your test isn't first thing in the morning, consider going for a walk or doing a light workout before the test to get your blood flowing.

Allow yourself enough time to get ready, and leave for the test with plenty of time to spare so you won't have the anxiety of scrambling to arrive in time. Another reason to be early is to select a good seat. It's helpful to sit away from doors and windows, which can be distracting. Find a good seat, get out your supplies, and settle your mind before the test begins.

When the test begins, start by going over the instructions carefully, even if you already know what to expect. Make sure you avoid any careless mistakes by following the directions.

Then begin working through the questions, pacing yourself as you've practiced. If you're not sure on an answer, don't spend too much time on it, and don't let it shake your confidence. Either skip it and come back later, or eliminate as many wrong answers as possible and guess among the remaining ones. Don't dwell on these questions as you continue—put them out of your mind and focus on what lies ahead.

Be sure to read all of the answer choices, even if you're sure the first one is the right answer. Sometimes you'll find a better one if you keep reading. But don't second-guess yourself if you do immediately know the answer. Your gut instinct is usually right. Don't let test anxiety rob you of the information you know.

If you have time at the end of the test (and if the test format allows), go back and review your answers. Be cautious about changing any, since your first instinct tends to be correct, but make sure you didn't misread any of the questions or accidentally mark the wrong answer choice. Look over any you skipped and make an educated guess.

Copyright © Mometrix Media. You have been licensed one copy of this document for personal use only. Any other reproduction or redistribution is strictly prohibited. All rights reserved.

At the end, leave the test feeling confident. You've done your best, so don't waste time worrying about your performance or wishing you could change anything. Instead, celebrate the successful completion of this test. And finally, use this test to learn how to deal with anxiety even better next time.

> **Review Video: 5 Tips to Beat Test Anxiety**
> Visit mometrix.com/academy and enter code: 570656

Important Qualification

Not all anxiety is created equal. If your test anxiety is causing major issues in your life beyond the classroom or testing center, or if you are experiencing troubling physical symptoms related to your anxiety, it may be a sign of a serious physiological or psychological condition. If this sounds like your situation, we strongly encourage you to seek professional help.

Copyright © Mometrix Media. You have been licensed one copy of this document for personal use only. Any other reproduction or redistribution is strictly prohibited. All rights reserved.

Thank You

We at Mometrix would like to extend our heartfelt thanks to you, our friend and patron, for allowing us to play a part in your journey. It is a privilege to serve people from all walks of life who are unified in their commitment to building the best future they can for themselves.

The preparation you devote to these important testing milestones may be the most valuable educational opportunity you have for making a real difference in your life. We encourage you to put your heart into it—that feeling of succeeding, overcoming, and yes, conquering will be well worth the hours you've invested.

We want to hear your story, your struggles and your successes, and if you see any opportunities for us to improve our materials so we can help others even more effectively in the future, please share that with us as well. **The team at Mometrix would be absolutely thrilled to hear from you!** So please, send us an email (support@mometrix.com) and let's stay in touch.

If you'd like some additional help, check out these other resources we offer for your exam:

http://MometrixFlashcards.com/CIA

Copyright © Mometrix Media. You have been licensed one copy of this document for personal use only. Any other reproduction or redistribution is strictly prohibited. All rights reserved.

Additional Bonus Material

Due to our efforts to try to keep this book to a manageable length, we've created a link that will give you access to all of your additional bonus material.

Please visit https://www.mometrix.com/bonus948/cia to access the information.

Copyright © Mometrix Media. You have been licensed one copy of this document for personal use only. Any other reproduction or redistribution is strictly prohibited. All rights reserved.